The Four Minsters Round the Wrekin

(40)

THE
Four Minsters Round the Wrekin:

BUILDWAS, HAUGHMOND, LILLESHULL AND WENLOCK,

WITH GROUND PLANS

BY

MACKENZIE E. C. WALCOTT, B.D., F.S.A.,

Præcentor and Prebendary of Chichester.

---✠---

"Ye holy walls that still sublime
"Resist the crumbling touch of Time,
"How strongly still your form displays
"The piety of former days."—BURNS.

---✠---

SHREWSBURY
ADNITT & NAUNTON, BOOKSELLERS, THE SQUARE.
LONDON·
SIMPKIN, MARSHALL, & Co., STATIONERS HALL COURT.

MDCCCLXXVII

To the Companion of my Life's Journey, these reminiscences of bright summer holidays are appropriately inscribed.

PREFACE.

*Res ardua vetustis novitatem dare, novis auctoritatem,
Obsoletis nitorem, obscuris lucem, fastiditis gratiam,
Dubus fidem.*
—*Plin. Hist Nat I Praf.*

THE class of books to which the present volume belongs command a large circulation, because they fulfil the requirements of a public, whom larger, more technical, and costly works fail to reach. It is of the highest importance, therefore, that they should not be produced by hasty, incompetent or partial writers, but prove means of conveying accurate, strictly truthful, and, if possible, new information

At the suggestion of MESSRS ADNITT AND NAUNTON, these pages were placed in their hands to supply a patent want, a memoir of the Four Minsters which lie within reach of the populous and much frequented town, I had almost said City, of Shrewsbury, for it once gave title to a bishop They were at first written for my own information, and collated on the spot. They have been subsequently supplemented by special research amongst the manuscripts of the Bodleian Library, Oxford, the British Museum, and Public Record Office, and topics of general as well as immediately local interest, like the authorities given in the side notes, have been thoughtfully selected. The great Benedictine Abbey of S. S Peter and Paul belongs essentially to the more particular history of the town.

To myself they are reminiscences of pleasant summer hours, to the inhabitants of Shrewsbury and the County I offer them as a true labour of love from a Salopian by descent, but my object in publication will be attained if they spread among an ever widening circle of readers a truer knowledge of the facts, with more of reverence and charity

Ruins are no fit subject for sentimental maundering, (sitting solitary as a widow bereft of her children, with all their beauty marred or departed), or cruel aspersions on their former inmates, the tongues which could have rebutted the calumny are silent in the grave · and like scars upon the country are these reverend buildings, wild and waste, profaned, dishonoured and defaced. Abuses, too great independence of supervision, decay of discipline within, and the change in the temper of the times led to their suppression but their lands mainly attracted the spoiler, and mammon drove out all nobler considerations; no pagan could have used them worse, they were not spared for holy use and the national benefit, as LATIMER pleaded but in vain, and to this hour we lament a marked decadence in the old spirit of reverence and devotion which followed upon the rude wrecking of these houses of God "It pitieth His servants to see them in the dust."

The ground whereon these consecrated structures were raised is still holy, and therefore no place for levity of speech and conduct, or for holiday amusements, much less for pastime

These unrestored memorials of the infinite taste and genius of our forefathers, who built for eternity, are very precious as a school of instruction, and should be regarded as national monuments Their inmates, whatever their shortcomings, kept the adjacent roads in repair, they maintained a generous entertainment when the vile hostelries were haunts of vice and robbers their knowledge of medicine and their alms benefitted the poor. peaceful pursuits, art and learning, and agriculture, spread their influence far and wide, and continual services offered an ever open house of prayer.

The careful preservation of these remains from demolition and wanton injury, and the stoppage of the progress of further decay materially conduce to the attractions and interest of their neighbourhood, and the good name of those persons into whose hands their safe keeping has devolved.

> Now ruin, beauty, and ancient stillness, all
> Dispose to judgments temperate as we lay
> On our past selves in life's declining day
> Perversely curious, then, for hidden ill
> Why should we break Time's charitable seals?
> Once ye were holy, ye are holy still,
> Your spirit let me freely drink and live —WORDSWORTH.

58, *Belgrave Road,*
    London, S W.

Buildwas Abbey from N.W.

From a Photograph by J. Laing, Shrewsbury

THE CISTERCIAN ABBEY

OF

S.S. MARY AND CHAD,

BUILDWAS.

---✠---

"The hills which bound the distant ken
"Banish the thoughts and feet of men,
"And make a solemn quiet here,
"So calm, so beautiful, so drear."—*I Williams*

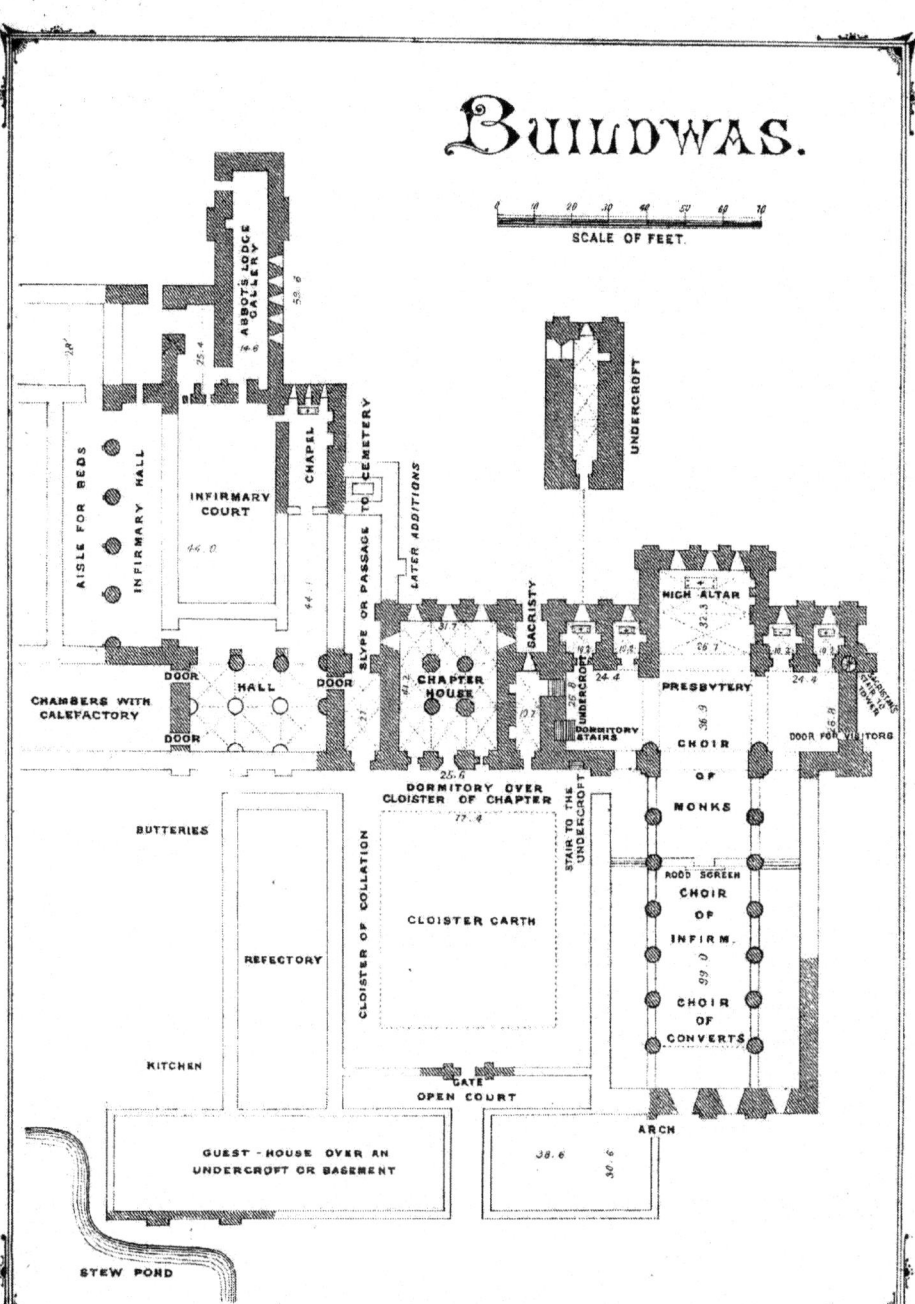

THE CISTERCIAN ABBEY OF S.S. MARY AND CHAD, BUILDWAS.

BUILDWAS is a name compounded of two words, *beuld*, a shelter, and *was*, an alluvial level, like Sugwas, Moccas, Rotherwas, Broadwas, and exactly expresses the position occupied by the abbey, which like others of the Cistercian order was dedicated to S Mary. A second saint, Chad of Lichfield, (no doubt added by the founder in honour of the mother Church of the diocese), is, however, commemorated just as S Edward is named in conjunction with the Blessed Virgin at Netley and Balmerino It is situated within an amphitheatre of wooded heights, with the Severn flowing on the north, in a secluded valley. A railway station is within a walk of ten minutes, and a portion of the domestic buildings is still habitable, and has been restored

In Domesday Beldewas, was is land formed by river floodings Old high German wass = caspes, modern German wassen, a grassy level, a surface of grass. Fr Caxon (Prof Earle)

THE ABBEY, ORIGINALLY SAVIGNIAC, BECOMES CISTERCIAN.

The abbey was founded Aug. 8, 1135, by Roger de Clinton, bishop of Chester, the Crusader. He it was who built the Castle and strengthened the

Eyton in Jo Arch Inst xv 319 334 Cotton MS, Faust B vii. fo 36 and Dodsworth MS ex Bodl Libr

ramparts of the city, augmented the capitular prebends of Lichfield Cathedral, and was one of the few Englishmen who sat in the Council of Lateran in 1139. It belonged to the Tyronensian or Savigniac branch of the order of Citeaux, like Furness, Calder, Burcester, Byland, Combermere, Dieulacres, Buckfastre, Quarr, Stratford, Stanlaw, Coggeshall, Jorvaulx, Neath, and Stanley.

> The Abbey of Savigny, fifteen leagues from Coutances, was founded in 1112 by Vital de Mortain, Chaplain to Earl Robert of Mortain, and Canon of S. Evroult, as a reformed branch of Benedictines; they eschewed meat, rarely drank wine, and lived upon oatmeal, pulse, cheese and honey; they slept on pallets of straw. In conjunction with them, Bernard de Abbeville founded S. Saviour's, Tiron, in 1114, equally austere, and consisting of a community of skilled workmen, labourers, artisans and husbandmen. Furness, in England, was built as a cell of Savigny in 1127. At length Serlo, abbot of Savigny, resigned his own house with its thirty-three dependent minsters into the hands of S. Bernard, abbot of Clairvaux, and P. Eugene III, by a bull dated April 11, 1148, confirmed the union with Citeaux. The grey monk of Savigny then assumed the white habit of the Cistercian.

Giraldus Cambrensis thus gives the history and ideal of the order of White Monks, so called in distinction from the black-frocked Benedictines. "Four Cluniacs of Sherborne, under one Harding, seeking to serve God after a more perfect way, went over the French Sea, and crossing the plain, reached Burgundy, a country wide and rough, full of woods and fertile in land; and twice they essayed to find a habitation. At length they found a rest which they therefore called "Cistercium,"* Citeaux, in 1098 Robert with twelve or twenty Monks from Molesme joined the new community. Their dress was of undyed wool, meat was allowed only in extreme sickness. Conspicuous for charity and hospitality their gates were never closed, morning noon nor night.

The desert was their home far from crowds, their food was won with the labour of their own hands; no furs, no hearth warmed their hardy limbs. They would have no rent from lands and manors, no parish churches or cure of souls"

ENDOWMENTS OF THE ABBEY

Between 1135 and 1145 Philip de Belmeis, the great benefactor of Lilleshall, gave Ruckley to the brotherhood of Buildwas and its mother Savigny. Before 1160 William Fitzalan added Holy Trinity Church, Little Buildwas; Cosford, St Mary's Leighton, and Hutton were later donations, in 1292 the dependent manors were Kynewerton (given in exchange for Conede Church), Wentnor with its mill, Rogden, and Hope Bowdler, in Hereford diocese, and in Lichfield—Walton, Brockton, and Cuddeston; their granges were at Wenbroke with a water mill, Ruckley, Stirchley, Monk's Mill, Bilton, Walton, and Brocketon; lands and rents produced two sums of £6 7s 10d. and £21 18s. 6d., live stock amounted to £9 10s. 0d. in value, the temporalities amounted to £113 19s 5d, in 1535/8 they were only £110 19s. 3½d., out of this they paid various vicars for ministering on outlying granges or farms, £20 to Counde for Harnage, to Idsall 16s for Hatton, 10s to Albrighton for Gofforde, and 5s. to Wentnor for Kynnerton. Possibly the exhibition of a cope wrought by the hands of Fair Rosamond may have attracted visitors with offerings and gifts to the fabric, but in 1406 Hugh Burnell was fain to bestow the advowson of Rushbury to compensate the convent for the losses which the burning of the Abbey Church by the Welsh had occasioned, so that the monks could not celebrate Divine Service. It is quite clear that the injury was confined to the destruction of the roofs

One of the most conspicuous benefactors was Philip de Broseley in

Eyton
vi 317
Val Eccles
III 191
Min Acc. 102.
27 28
Hen viii
Chirbury.
m. 7
Harl MS
2060.

1220, who allowed the monks to quarry stone, and, by order of the King in 1235, empowered them to cut wood in Shirlot Forest in order to complete their buildings, when some alterations still perceptible were made in the eastern arm of the church. The monks had a town house in Lichfield granted by Bishop Hugh. They were slow in giving to royal necessities, for Prynne tells an anecdote of an abbot of Buildwas being summoned hastily to Court and roughly questioned by Henry III. "How comes it that you refuse money to my humble suit in my poverty? Am I not your patron, father and protector?" "Yes," retorted the abbot," but it befits not your majesty to ruin us by extortion, but rather like the pious King of the Franks to ask our prayers." "I want both," said the King, "money and prayers." "Sire," said the churchman," "that is impossible I wis, one or the other is at your service, but not both together."

DEPENDENT ABBEYS.

In 1152 the abbot of Savigny gave over to Buildwas the charge of Basingwerk Abbey. In 1174 Henry II. ratified the grant. In 1177, and again in 1192, the Flintshire daughter tried to assert her independence, but successive abbots of Savigny—William of Toulouse, Richard de Curci, and Arnold—refused the claim. On Nov. 26, 1156, to Buildwas was assigned by Savigny the care of St. Mary's, Dublin, founded in 1138, which chose a Buildwas monk, Roger de Brugor, as their superior in the 14th century.

On one occasion the abbey received a charge which it was glad to repudiate on prudential grounds. Harvey de Montemarisco bestowed Dunbrody on our abbey, but Allan, one of the monks who went over to see the gift, found it waste and bare, so Buildwas very prudently transferred the seigneury to S. Mary's at Dublin, and in 1342 the convent renewed this grant.

S. Mary's, Port S. Mary, Co Wexford, was a cell of Buildwas, which also had the right of visitation in the reign of Edward III. over the Welch abbey of Strat-Marcell.

THE ABBOTS.

Ingenulf.

Ranulf, c 1156, died on his journey to Savigny in 1182. He and the prior of Wallingford, afterwards abbot of Malmsbury, were the only Conventual superiors who as adventurers, accompanied Henry II in his invasion of Ireland.

Robert c. 1182.

William I.

Uchtred c 1210.

Stephen c. 1227

Simon c. 1233

Nicholas c 1236-1256.

William II. c 1263.

Alan or Adam c. 1271.

Gilbert de Lacy c 1291

William III c. 1292

The abbot of Buildwas was summoned to Parliament 31, Edward I.
Henry Burnell.

John Burnell c. 1317

Nicholas or Nathanael c 1347.

John Leigh c. 1406

Henry Derby c. 1453

William Wulley c. 1474.

Sir Richard Emery

1520 Stephen Grene. He resigned on a pension of £16, with 12 monks, who received nothing.

Blakeway MS fo 78 Eyton's List. Duke's MS List.

VI. 333

(Stevens App II p 12)

Misc Book Augm Off 232 P 1 fo. 41

It was not until a later date that the deprived conventual members received a pension, probably in those evil days of oppression and spoil, in deference to the silent effect of public opinion, which had been outraged by scenes of sacrilege The general grant of pensions together with actual promotion of Monks and regular Canons in the new foundations invalidate the falsehoods and perversions put forth by the royal commissioners

The following payments were made in 1553 —

<small>Exch Q R
Misc Books
32 fo. xlviii</small>

    Bwyldwas,   Will Charlton, xx*s*
    Annuities,   Stephen Pelle, xxvi*s*. viii*d*
    and *Corrodies*, Edw Lakyn, c*s*

These were the last payments to the numerous pensioners fastened upon religious houses by Kings, patrons, and persons of power resident in the vicinity, many of whom also held salaried offices as chief steward, auditor and the like The cost often taxed the revenues to one-tenth of their amount

<small>Pa Ro 29
Hen viii
P 1 m 30
(6)</small>

One volume out of the Library, a M.S. treatise on the Apocalypse, is preserved in the Library of Shrewsbury School. The site, with bell tower and church on July 4, 1537, passed to Edward Grey Lord Powys In 1617 it was purchased by Thomas Lord Ellesmere, then it was sold to Sir William Acton of London, from whom it has descended in the female line to the Moseleys of the Mere, Co Stafford, since the reign of Charles II.

THE ABBEY CHURCH.

Possibly before the Suppression the straitened revenues and diminished community had caused many an eventful change in the appearance of the

Buildwas Abbey, looking East.

From a Photograph by J. Laing, Shrewsbury.

church and cloistral buildings, but the brutal hand of desecration has dismantled the low lantern tower, thrown down the groined roof of the sanctuary, torn up the pavement of tiles, swept away the upper walls of the transept, and left only a bare avenue of two arcades reaching from the west end to the tower.

The plan of the building is cruciform 163 feet long, and in the main 26 feet 8 inches in breadth   The nave is 70 feet including five bays   the ritual choir including the two remaining bays and the crossing 62 feet the Presbytery which is square ended and aisleless 34 ft. by 26ft 9in., and the Transept with two chapels to each wing, as at Kirkstall, separated by solid walls, 84 ft.

<small>Potter's Specim 1848. Memoirs by Rev J L. Petit, Jo Arch Inst xv, 335 344, G M Hills in Collect Brit Arch. Assoc., Britton's Archit Antiq iv, and J Buckler in Add. MS 27 765</small>

THE NAVE.

The pillars of the Nave are single, massive, round, and seven on each side, symbolical of the verse in the Proverbs of Solomon, "Wisdom hath builded an House . she hath hewn out her seven pillars." They suggest the true idea of a sombre church with an unearthly solemnity, reared by a silent rugged brotherhood, conversing by means of an elaborate code of manual signs, stern in their austere life, hard, spare diet, and unintermitted bodily labour   In their Minster a few lamps only relieved the gloom, like that now pervading the sanctuary and chapels in the deep grey obscurity of twilight, the simple colour of the stone sufficed, a single cross or rood marked the place as holy, no living imagery, no company of saintly figures clustered round and seemed like angels on a heavenly stair—ascending and descending on the tiers of a sumptuous reredos ; no splendid shrines raised a fretwork of gold or glittered with ruby, sapphire, emerald, and pearls of the East. no gorgeous screens fenced the simple altar with its twin pale tapers, and vessels of precious metal wrought as plain as the craftsmen could frame them, glass of a cold pearly

<small>Prov ix 1</small>

hue filled the small windows; a knot of delicate foliage witnessed to the intense love of nature in these hardy men who lived their days more in the woods and fields, vocal with the song of birds and the sounds of animated nature, than in the cloister, silent as the grave, and cheered their lowly toil with sentences descriptive of rural beauty, culled from their favourite book the Song of Solomon a solitary bell, or at most two, rang slow and mournful calls to Matins and Evensong, to Mass and Angelus. The worship was as cold in outward form as it was frequent in celebration, and therefore in no Minster fallen from its sacred use to desolation can we less take to heart the lifelike touching picture drawn of old by an inspired hand, which described a ruined house of God as "a lodge in a garden."

The label mouldings of the nave are continuous resting upon the capitals. The rood-screen was erected to enclose the second bays of the nave reckoning from the lantern. The two eastern pillars, 18 inches shorter than the rest, are accommodated to receive the choir stalls, one on the south side is octagonal, that which faces it consists of a semicircle and semioctagon combined The late Norman capitals are square, as at Tewkesbury, Gloucester, and Southwell, with indented angles, delicately treated and of the cushion type The bases of the choir pillars are massive and more raised than those in the nave, but they all terminated their base mouldings and chamfered plinths against the interrupting wall towards the aisles The arches are Pointed with plain orders, the clerestory is deeply splayed within broad steep sills, the windows have shafts with delicately sculptured capitals It has a corbel table, and flat pilaster buttresses, as the case was probably also in the aisle Two lofty windows, separated by a flat buttress, fill the west end of the nave, elevated, as at Kirkstall, as if intended at first to admit beneath them a portal which was never made. The number of putlog holes in the sides of old churches which puzzle strangers, were prepared for the scaffolding whilst the walls were being carried up, and

Bui

were often not filled up, as in Cymmer Abbey, near Dolgelley, presenting thus an unsightly assemblage of apertures. Here the preparations made for an inner porch constructed of timber are still visible it consisted of a gallery over a timber structure below It formed a useful communication between the aisles, and a boundary to the people, who were permitted to go along either side towards the sanctuary without passing up the nave or choir. Here it occupied one bay in depth and screened off the western couplet It appears to have been an addition in the 15th Century, but may have replaced the earlier closure of the lay brothers who always sat at the west end At Byland, Fountains, and Tintern there was an outer longitudinal Galilee-porch

The rood-screen completely separated the nave from the choir the screen of stone reaching 3 feet above the capitals, communicated with the dwarf side walls 7 feet wide and 2 feet broad, which filled up all the arches of the nave towards either aisle The upper gallery was of wood and uncanopied, and its frame was fixed above the cornice of the clerestory At Tintern portions of such walls cling to the pillars, and traces remain at Cleeve and Valle Crucis They had a plain coping sloped only on the inside A second screen midway in the nave has been discovered at Fountains They mark the threefold distinction lengthwise into the choir of the Monks, the choir of the Infirm, and the choir of Converts or lay brothers

<small>See my Memoir on Cleeve Abbey in the Proc. of the Roy Inst of Brit Arch 1876</small>

The crossing had no side walls at the back of the choir stalls of oak. The broad arches of the Lantern spring from corbels high up in the walls, three arches only have labels where they would be seen from the west The angles of the pillars entering the transept are faced with pillars having capitals with various ornaments of the 12th Century The east and west arches, slightly pointed spring from elongated corbels The Lantern had two small

c

windows on each side, and was reached by stairs at the S.E. angle, through the roof of the chapels

The Transept has in each wing two chapels entered under a pointed arch, They have groins with diagonal ribs which sprang as at Valle Crucis from corbels in the angles, and were built under the vault Each chapel has a plain Norman window : and measures 11ft. 3in. by 10ft. 2in on the south, and 10ft 8in by 10ft 5in on the north.

The South Wing had a stone staircase jutting from its eastern angle which led to the Lantern Westward of it was a fine doorway 4ft. 9in wide A corresponding staircase occurs at Valle Crucis. The inner chapel next the Presbytery had an arched aumbry, opposite to it is another recessed locker, and at its foot a piscina on a taper corbel-bracket. The South Chapel has a similar adjunct of the Altar.

The Chapels in the North Wing have the same design and accessories. In the North Wall, on the west side, is the aperture for a door 4ft. 10in wide, and 8ft above the pavement, through which the Monks descended by stairs from the Dormitory for the night hours. Remains of the original cement coating upon the walls are here visible. On the east side, at either end of a deep and vaulted recess six feet in depth, are two doorways which formed a passage from the transept to the Sacristy between it and the Chapter House, which lay at a lower level of five feet.

THE PRESBYTERY was completely screened off like the choir, and no light streamed westward from its windows. In the 15th Century the two tiers of its eastern lancet windows were formed into a triplet in a single height, and the south window was elongated as at Llanthony and Brinkburne being cut down to the same level. The altar was also detached from the east wall.

THE SEDILIA, or seats for the celebrant and his assistants, supplanted early in the 13th Century the Norman bench. These are three in number, and deeply recessed, divided by slender pillars, and the capitals and arches have the beautiful violet or four-leaved ornament. The piscina, or water drain for the ablutions, between the sedilia and elongated window, and the aumbry are original; the former is a plain, round headed recess, 3ft. wide. The aumbry was partially destroyed by the elongation of the adjoining window. The corresponding window on the north has happily escaped defacement, and is in a line with the clerestory. The eastern arm was groined in stone in two bays, the ribs springing from corbels of singular shape, with small side pillars and carved capitals.

THE UNDERCROFT OF THE TRANSEPT.

The basement of the northern bay of the transept has a semi-crypt-like appearance, but originally it was less underground than it is. There are somewhat similar structures below altar platforms in the south nave aisles of Dorchester an Austin Canons' Church, and the Collegiate Minster of Bosham. Over its vault to a height of more than two feet it has a raised platform of solid stone. The only entrance is by steps from the cloister; the main wall of the transept in front of the eastern chapel crosses the vault upon an arch. Two bays, divided by an arch springing from corbels, complete the chamber. The slope of the ground in a northerly direction necessitated the peculiar formation; the floor is on a level with that of the chapter-house, that is, five feet lower than the level of the choir. The oak door, a very ancient one, has no lock, all the bands and fastenings of iron are on the inside, a fact which points to its occasional use as the Parlour for official conversation. The ancient plaster remains over the rough mason work beneath its smooth surface. The arches have a very slight pointed form. There is an east window made into a doorway, and a north window in the upper bay, they were probably closed with wooden shutters. In the south wall is a Norman arch over a seat. The object of the room was probably to contain the cowls laid aside by the monks in going to their daily work, but here also may have been laid the departed brother on his bier, with a single watcher by turns reciting the Psalter whilst sitting beside him

THE CLOISTER GARTH OR ENCLOSURE

The Cloister was the place in which the whole inner and home life was spent by such monks as had no special office and duties during the hours not allotted to devotion, field work, meals and sleep. It is placed on the north side owing to its proximity to the river, as at Tintern and Melrose, necessities of the site also fixed the claustral range in this position at Ford, Dore in the Golden Valley, Balmerino, and Beauport (c. 1202) which greatly resembles the whole arrangement of Buildwas the case was the same in the Austin Canons' houses of Worksop and Hexham, in the Benedictine Monasteries of Canterbury, Gloucester, Sherborne, and Chester, and the secular Cathedrals of Lincoln and S David's

De Caumont Abec p 26 88 90

THE WEST SIDE OF THE CLOISTER GARTH

Duke's MS fo 119 My plans in Add MS, Brit Mus 29 540

Was enclosed by a wall as at Beaulieu, Tintern, Byland, Dore, Boyle, and Netley, and pierced by a gateway of four orders with nookshafts and chevroned mouldings, which fell down in 1820 On the outer side projecting beyond the west front was the Guest House, over cellarage, as at Beaulieu, Byland, Kirkstall, Fountains, and Cleeve. This chamber was also known as the Ostrey or Hostry The alley next the Church was called the "Reading Cloister." Persons who came as worshippers, and not as guests, entered by the door in the south front of the Transept, and were accommodated in the retro-choir, the part of the nave-aisle, which was behind the stalls.

<small>Claustrum Collacionis</small>

The Refectory appears to have lain parallel to the Church, as at Whalley, Cleeve, Robertsbridge, Croxden, Merevale, Waverley, Furness, Neath, Balmerino, Dunbrody, Boyle, and five French abbeys, including Pontigny, and not at right angles Whilst the north and west ranges of buildings have been rased to the ground, the eastern portion has been preserved, even to its stone vaulting It measures 62 feet, and includes the Sacristy, the Chapter House and a Slype or thoroughfare passage.

<small>Frater at Hayles & Dieulacres

Augm Off Books 494 fo 71, 172 fo 41</small>

THE SACRISTY

The Sacristy or Vestry between the Chapter House and Transept, entered from under a segmental arch, is 10ft. 6in. wide, the floor being below that of the Cloister. It is vaulted and groined in two bays formed by an arch across the centre; the springers rest on huge plain corbels In the north wall there are two recesses with plain Norman arches. These lockers or aumbries for books used in cloister time are 3ft. 2in. wide, 2ft. 4in. deep, and 4ft. high, and perfectly plain The east window has been broken into a doorway. On the south side there is a door communicating with the transept by a flight of five stairs

THE CHAPTER HOUSE

The Chapter House is oblong, 41ft 6in by 31ft. 6in. It is groined upon four slender pillars The NE and SW are octagonal, the others placed diagonally to them are round All the capitals are octagonal, the two on the north plain, the other pair ornamented. The vault is formed of stone slabs Portions of the plaster remain upon it and on the side walls. The floor is sunk in order to give sufficient altitude to the chamber, without sacrifice of height in the upper storey Three windows at the east end facing the alleys, and one in each side wall form those piercings so common in the early Cistercian Sanctuary and Chapter House as symbolical of the five Wounds of the Crucifixion. It contains several 13th century coffins with beautiful crosses Some tiles (now in the dwelling-house) are of great variety, and bear the arms of the Spencers, and Lombardic letters, relics of sepulchral inscriptions. The entrance Portal is deeply recessed, two shafts with scollopped capitals flanked it on either side, and two unglazed windows complete the front, in richness of chevroned decoration, and with a pair of shafts on their outer face and on the sides, they excelled the central doorway which never received the ornament which doubtless was in the intention of the first builders. A continuous label, however, slightly modifies the absence of decoration, ingeniously contrived, like steps ascending or descending to unite the detached members in one harmonious elevation The cloister alleys were covered with a pent roof, straight, and resting on a front without windows or doors, and no special care was taken to raise it before the Chapter House. In this Chamber the daily chapter was held for reading the rule and martyrology, with commemmoration of the dead, and for infliction of penance, and, if necessary, actual discipline with the scourge

SLYPE TO THE CEMETERY

Northward of the Chapter House, the Slype, or open Passage, is 10ft wide, groined in stone in two bays, with moulded ribs and arches. The springers and corbels resemble those in the adjoining chamber The entrance has a single pillar on each side The under arch is segmental

The whole range northward of the Transept formed the substructure of the Dormitory, and from the number of windows lighting separate cells, a close approximation is made to the number also of the members of the community Only one window remains, but a few fragments of those which are missing may be traced along the upper line of the wall. Buck, in 1731, represents seven, and three more at least must have lighted this side, giving twenty in all At the dissolution there were twelve monks

Dorter at Dieulacres, Whalley, etc Ch Ho. Books A.⅜ fo 182

THE HALL OR BASEMENT

The building next the Slype, forming part of the substructure of the the Dormitory was divided into three bays in either direction; the eastern alley communicated on the south with the Chapel, and on the north with the Infirmary. This building formed the Hall, and in it those occupations which ordinarily took place in the cloister were carried on, when inclement weather rendered work impossible in the exposed alleys, barely sheltered by a roof The usual position of the Hall is at the extremity of the eastern or western range, and the exterior windows were left unglazed and unshuttered, so that the monks might be working as if still in the open air. The capitals of the round pillars are square, but the scollopped ornaments resemble those in the Church. In the south wall there is a recess 2ft. 8in. wide, and in the opposite

Augm Off Books 172 fo 6 42

angle of the north wall, a broken doorway, as it would seem, which may have led into another chamber, probably the Calefactory or Common House, on the north side.

The position of the principal buildings was no doubt observed by an unwritten canon, the Church lying parallel to the Refectory, the Chapter House and Slype on the east side, and the Dormitory connected with the transept, but there was no prescriptive authority for the arrangement of the subordinate structures and offices, including the Copyists' room, the Library usually over or near the Chapter House, the novices' rooms, and the lodgings of the lay brothers (sometimes near the west alley) before their transmission to the outlying farms or granges, whence they only came in on Sunday to attend mass, hence the difficulty which is experienced in allotting the lesser chambers to their definite purpose Here on the north-east side of the Great Cloister we have a second Court of the Infirmary, one of the most important features in a monastery as it usually contained about one-third of the community who had become invalided through age or sickness

THE INFIRMARY

On the south side of the Infirmary Court there was a long building, the western half (now destroyed with the exception of a weather-moulding on the east side of the Undercroft), formed an outer hall or nave, the eastern part was a Chapel, of the Transition period, 15 feet broad A Norman cornice extends along the south wall, which contains a recessed seat for the celebrant, and an aumbry for the vessels of the altar under a semicircular stone covered with carved work of Norman foliage in low relief

The Hall of the Infirmary, erected before the close of the 12th century, forming the north side of this Quadrangle, and the earliest portion in the pure Pointed style, is now represented by an arcade in five bays, which originally divided two collateral alleys measuring 76 × 30 feet. The pillars are short and round, but of smaller diameter than in the nave; the capitals are circular and moulded, and the arches are more sharply pointed, all significant of the Transitional period. On the north side of each pillar is a slender stone bracket, once richly carved, 20in. long, provided for lamps which lighted the beds of the infirm in the outer alley, the inner aisle was their Table Hall. It was entered by two doors opening from the Infirmarer's lodging, one of them has been altered in the 14th century. On the east side of the Infirmary Court is a two storeyed building, the upper rooms being approached by a flight of stone steps which abut on the Chapel wall, and through a plain pointed doorway, but it has been miserably patched, altered and mutilated. It formed the lodging of the Infirmarer and his assistants, and contained two lower parlours, divided by a partition of stone. On the south side is a gallery 59ft 8in. × 14ft, which opened into the Infirmary Court, and communicates with the adjoining chamber. It retains five windows towards the west end and an ancient ceiling of stout timber scantling. The entrance to the next room has slender pillars on the sides.

De Caumont Abec p 26, 88 90.

A stone archway on the upper floor led to the chambers over the north wing of the Infirmary, in order to avoid the multiplication of inner staircases, and as an additional provision for security. Over the south room were, probably, the abbot's chambers marked by a southern gable, pierced with a couplet, over which was a trefoil, and on either side a lancet window. It was lighted by five side windows. The ceiling is of the 15th century. Whatever may have been the practice in later times, Ralph de Coggeshall distinctly

D

<small>Chron p. 134</small>   mentions a Cistercian Abbot who said:—"It is not our custom to receive guests in our private rooms, but to dine with them in hall."

<small>Blakeway MS. fo 78</small>   This portion of the remains has been lately "restored," and many ancient features are now almost undistinguishable. The fretwork ceiling once bore the portcullis, three ostrich feathers, and a heart inscribed Jesu.

<small>Harrod's Gleanings, p. 116</small>   One chamber, the Calefactory or room with a fireplace, used for providing light for the Sacristan, kindling charcoal for the censers, drying boots and parchments, and for warming cold limbs, cannot be definitely pointed out, it probably occupied a place north of the Undercroft. Towards the close of the 15th century fireplaces were introduced into the dormitories and halls of the once hardy Cistercians. Every monastery has its own individuality, and absolute precision in allotment of the chambers of the prior and sub-prior and the like, is quite beyond attainment owing to constant changes effected both before and after the suppression and the absence of official surveys.

> Into their cloisters now they broken had,
> Through which the Monks they chaced here and there,
> And then pursued them into their Dortors said,
> And searched all their cells and secrets near.
> From thence into the sacred Church they broke,
> And robbed the chancel, and the desks down threw,
> And altars spoiled and blasphemy spoke.

The walls shook out their inmates, lands once sown were left seedless, the full storehouses, granges, and stalls were emptied, darkness and silence fell on everything, the robbers entered in and defiled the holy place, "despoiling all with might and main," and a thoroughfare was made across the Church below the lantern, and so it continues to this day.

On Sundays admission is not permitted.

Haughmond Abbey from S.W.

From a Photograph by J. Laing, Shrewsbury

THE AUSTIN CANONS' ABBEY

OF

S John The Evangelist,

HAUGHMOND.

---✠---

" To forswear the full stream of the World and to
" live in a nook purely Monastick."
As You Like It

Vaughmond Abbey.

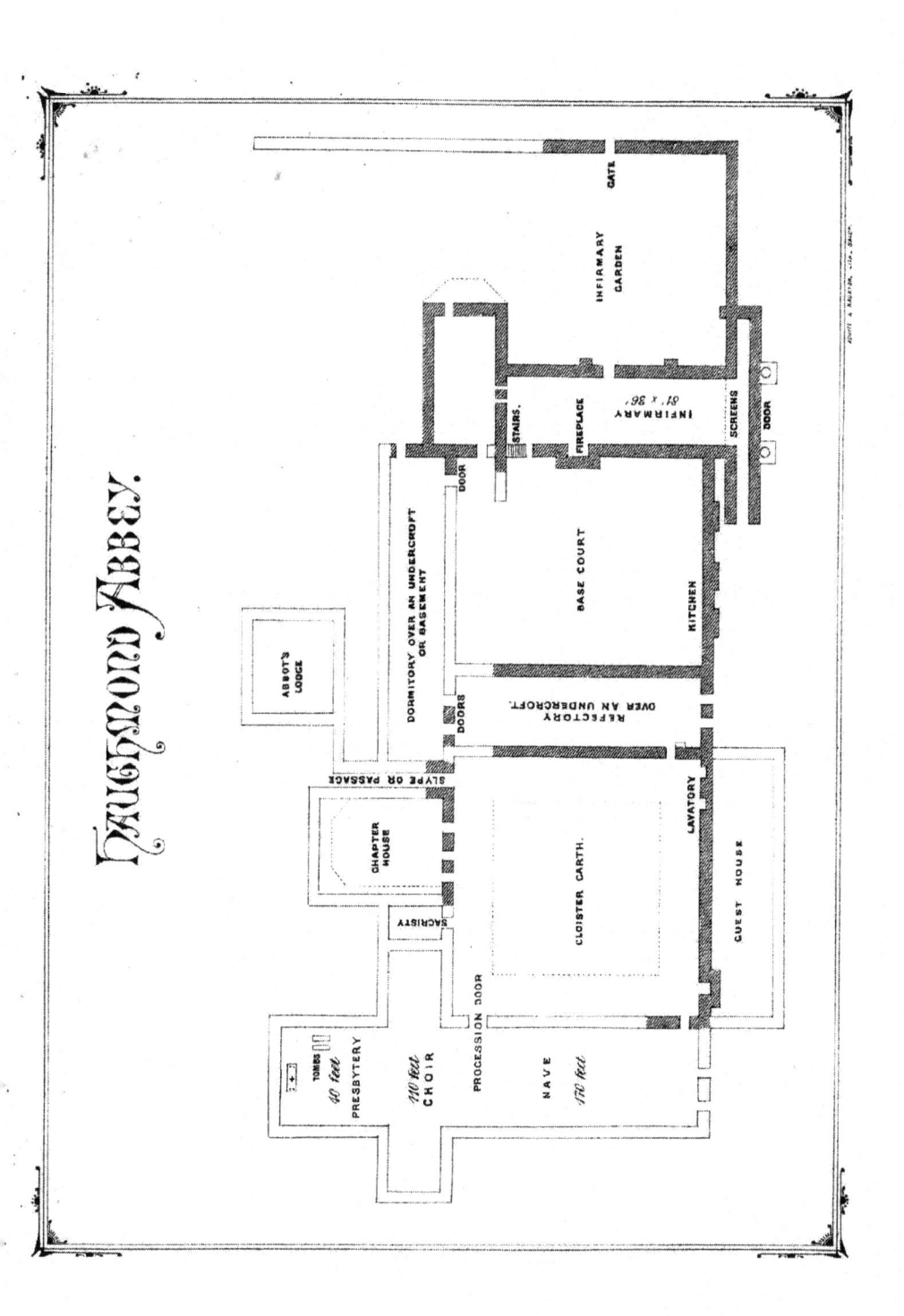

The Abbey of S. John the Evangelist, Haughmond.

HAUGHMOND ABBEY lies away from railroads, and is accessible only by a carriage or on foot. The road, four miles in length, leads under the Railway Bridge along the Castle Foregate, through the suburb, and about a quarter of a mile beyond S Michael's Church the grey masses of the abbey will be seen on the right, environed by trees, and sheltered by the wooded hill of Haughmond, which was the origin of its name Haughmond is *High Mound*, either A.S. *heah* and *munt*, or French, *Haut mont*, but probably the former. Haughmond Hill is a mere reduplication as in Richmond Hill.

At the distance of a mile, a road on the right hand of Old Heath turnpike must be taken, which passes by Sundorne Castle, and commands fine views of the rounded height of the Wrekin, Caradoc with its soaring peak, the Brown Clee, the noble brow of the Titterstone, the Long Mynd, Stipper Stones, and other lofty hills on either side of the beautiful and fertile valley that stretches under their shadows southward to Ludlow, the great mountainous chain that bounds England and Wales, Moel-y-Golphon, Cefn-y-Castel and the Breiddens, the silvery windings of the Severn among green pastures or golden corn fields, and beyond the meadows the clear, bright spires of the Churches of S. Mary and S. Alkmund, the Castle Towers, and the ruddy, picturesque buildings of Shrewsbury.

In one part when passing the lake at Sundorne a cool, shady avenue of trees is worthy of being transferred to the sketcher's book. A gentle rise now forms the approach to the abbey, seated on a slight eminence, once part of the royal forest of Mount Gilbert, and a tall gable flanked with turrets, gives a vain promise that the Minster still stands. One fragment only survives, and the outlines can scarcely be traced by the green mounds which mark the boundary foundations; the lofty tower, the solemn nave, the glorious choir have been swept clean from the earth, and all that they contained is scattered and lost. Long neglect has completed the sacrilegious work of demolition, and the site lies naked and waste, uncared for, overgrown with weeds, and dangerous with pitfalls and holes. Pity it is that there is no one, who has the power, with interest enough to preserve the few but precious fragments that remain

The great scene of demolition was forecast by the author of Pier's Ploughman's Creed —

> "And there shall come a King,
> And confess you Religious,
> And beat you, as the Bible teacheth,
> For breaking of your Rule,
> And amend morals,
> Monks and canons,
> Then shall the Abbot and all his issue for ever
> Have a knock of a King,
> And incurable the wound."

Harl' MS.
446, 2188
fol. 123)
3866 fo 11.

The abbey was founded upon the site of a hermitage and chapel, as a Priory for Austin or Black Canons (thus distinguished by the colour of their habit from the White or Premonstratensian Canons of Hales Owen) between 1130 and 1138 by William Fitz-Alan, who was buried not here but in the Abbey Church of SS. Peter and Paul at Shrewsbury. Sometime later, about the year 1155, it was raised to the honours of an abbey, when the founder bestowed upon it S Andrew's Church, Wroxeter; and, in order to provide a full convent, Walchelyn de Maminot gave (and William Peverall confirmed it) Bradford Mill, adding that of Upton in 1160 The Empress Matilda and the Stuarts were also benefactors. K. Stephen bestowed Walcot Mill. A papal bull in 1162 mentions as dependent churches S Mary's de Sissarcs and St. Michael's Trafegulus, Bangor diocese The noble family of le Zouche and Hugh de Say added Rochesford Mill. Helias de Say gave mills at Stokes and Watlinton; John le Strange gave Stretton Mill super Avenam, and the churches of S Mary Hunstanton, and S. Swithin Cheswardin; from William Fitz-Alan came All Saints Stoke-super-Teyrn, from Wido de Sauberià Sagbery (Shawbury, S Mary's) Church, in the reigns of Henry II and of the Edwards, S Andrew's, Stanton-super-Henheth; S. John Baptist's Ruyton, Hanmere, S. George's Pontesbury, S. Mary's Newyn, S Mary's Sellatyn, Lydurn, All Saints' Grinsell, and S. Mary's Lebotwood, were added, along with a market at Le Lye in Bodewode, Sundorne and Homebarn Granges, fisheries in the Severn, Walcote Manor, and other lands, woods and parks At the dissolution the net revenues amounted to £259 13s 7d

Lansdown MS 229, fol 104, 160, 250 Min Acc Publ. Off 126 Churbury A 30 and 31 Henry 8, m 14, Val Eccles 111 197, Fyton vii, 282

The Black Canons Regular of St Augustine so called in distinction to the White Canons of Premontré, lived in strict community as regulars, and so differed from secular Canons of Cathedral and Collegiate Churches, who maintained separate households. They were introduced at S. Oswald's, Nostell, and Carlisle Cathedral by Athelwolph, confessor to Henry I. Their principal houses were Colchester, St. Mary Overye, Smithfield, Dunstable, Kenilworth, Cirencester, Oseney, Oxford, Bristol, Worksop, and Waltham. The Clugniacs came to England before them, but the Canons of Auroise, the Savigniacs, the Cistercians, and the Premonstratensians were later in date. They wore a linen rochet under an open, black cope, and boots like monks, and not shoes as did secular canons.

<small>Reyner Apost Bened 1, 158, Lyndwood Prov Lib III, t 20, p 213</small>

The Priory of S. Mary's De Sartis at Raunton, Co Stafford, founded by Robert Fitz-Noel in the time of Henry II., was subordinate to Haughmond

THE MINSTER.

Until a complete survey of the site has been made with mattock and pickaxe, it is impossible to say more than this, that the Church was cruciform with a Lady Chapel, in which Sir Richard de Leatun founded a wax light to burn during the Lady Mass "on the midst of the beam there." There were also two chapels of S Anne and S. Andrew. By a special indulgence Pope Alexander III. in 1172 allowed the community in the time of a general interdict to say mass in a low voice, and within closed doors. The Churches of the Order of Austin Canons, who held an intermediate position between the stricter conventual order of monks, and the less rigid and uncloistered secular canons of Cathedral and Collegiate Churches, are reducible to several classes. Some, and with them Haughmond may be identified, were designed on a grand scale and with regular development, like Christchurch Hants, Cartmel, Worksop, Smithfield, Thornton, Llanthony, Bridlington, Southwark, Waltham, S Andrew's N.B , S German's, and Oseney ; others were less shapely, like Bristol, Dorchester, Walsingham, Newark, Oxford and Carlisle ; some, principally in the Northern and Midland Counties, had only a north nave aisle, as

<small>Blakeway MS, II fo 245 Bodl Lib Oxford, Harl MS 3868 fo 286</small>

Hexham, Ulvescroft, Bolton, Brinkburne, Newstead, Lanercost and Kirkham, whilst, as we shall see, Lilleshall was destitute of aisles. Here the discovery of Norman shafts of arcaded walls and a doorway on the N.W. side proves the the existence of at least an aisle on the north side of the nave From the steep slope of the ground grand flights of stairs probably led up at intervals and various stages to the high altar, as in Ashburnham Church and Finchale

A fragment of the S.W. portion of the Church has been preserved On its inner face there is a large round arch with nook-shafts banded at mid-height, above the cloister door, with the jambs of an arched window to the east of it. On the south side the actual round-headed Procession doorway, c 1150, is of three orders enriched with foliage and a truncated diamond ornament Between the shafts are canopied figures of SS. Peter and Paul, five feet high, probably additions of the 14th century The nave formed (as was usual with this order) a parish Church, and at the close of the 12th century one of the canons was empowered to act as Sacristan to minister sacraments to all the servants and members of the household, and to baptize infants and Jews. The patterns of twelve tiles forming the pavement have been preserved, they had red, chocolate, blue or yellow for the ground and various designs, some geometrical, some ornamented with foliage, one had concentric rings and rays like a web, and another was armorial with this charge, *or* a raven, and a third the mystic fish within an aureole

<small>Duke's MS fo 270,</small>

The transept had two bays in each wing, and the west side had a clerestory of three lofty, round-headed windows. The eastern arm was square-ended, and contains two monumental slabs incised with trefoiled crosses, which rise out of shields, they bear the following inscriptions —

<small>Duke's MS fo 243</small>

I.—Vous Ki Passez Par Ici Priez Pur L'Alme Johan Fitz Alcine Ki Git Ici Deu De Sa Alme Eit Merci. Amen.

<small>Duke's MSS fo 269 Bodl Lib Oxford</small>

E

*II —Isabel De Mortimer Sa Femme Acost De Li   Deu De Lur
Alme Eit Merci   Amen.*

<small>Gent Mag
xcv p 1
p 497</small>

They commemorate John Fitz Alan, lord of Clun, great grandson of the founder, and Isabel, Daughter of Roger, earl of Wigmore   He died in 1270   His widow married for the third time in 1285.   The Dedication of the Conventual Church to S John Evangelist is rare and beautiful, the greatest minsters bear the names of SS Peter and Paul, separately or in conjunction, Cologne, Toledo, Rome, York, and London, pre-eminently setting the example, the Blessed Virgin is commemmorated in every Cistercian house, at Lincoln, Salisbury, Seville, Palermo, Lisbon, Amiens, Strasburg, and Paris ; S Stephen, at Vienna and Mayence, S. Mark, at Venice, S. Ambrose at Milan, and local saints had an abundant share of honour, but, with the exception of Lyons, the title of the gentle Apostle of Love, the Seer of the Apocalypse, has rarely been bestowed upon a principal Church, the Lateran is dedicated to the two Saints John

THE CONVENTUAL BUILDINGS

The cloister garth occupies its normal position on the south side of the church   The west wall is complete, and runs even with the front of the Minster, it is battlemented throughout its extent, heavy folds of ivy concealing its decay.   This crenellation may have been added in the 15th century, when an outer building may have been removed   At the N.W angle is a large arch with nook shafts and capitals wrought with foliage. The inner arch, now filled up with a window, once, very possibly, communicated with some external range, like those of Hexham and Lanercost, as there is a curious corbelled projection on the outer wall, but there are no indications of a roof. When the numbers of the canons and the buildings were alike contracted before the suppression, and the outer range here was removed, this archway may have been formed with its deep recess into a cell for the usher or doorkeeper, or perhaps a seat for the superintendent of studies, the adjacent north alley of the cloister being devoted to the use of readers. At the south-west end there is a beautiful Lavatory, as at Kirkham and Hexham, (and in Benedictine Westminster and Norwich) formed of two large arches of two orders, with coupled lateral shafts, and supported on a central group of tripled shafts, with capitals wrought in foliage. It was once—

> Y paved with peyntil (tiles) each point after other,
> With conduits of clean tin, closed all about,
> With lavers of latten lovely y-greithed (adorned)

On the south side we find a portion of the Refectory which was erected over a substructure, to which a Pointed doorway gave access on the west. On the north side it is flanked by an obtuse arch and by one round-headed to the south. The only other undercrofts of Refectories occur in the Benedictine halls of Durham and Dunfermline, and the Cistercian Rievaulx and Cleeve Shrewsbury also had one. The west wall of the Refectory shows the lower part of a fine Perpendicular window of five lights, with two round-headed aumbries for plate and table furniture on the north of it, and a small arch with nook shafts, which formed part of an arcading on the south side. The north wall retains the jambs of the door which led from the cloister; it was shafted, banded at midheight, and of three orders, full of dignity when perfect. The south wall retains a small window and a large round-headed arch; on the outer wall there are two round-headed arches In its original state it was—

> An hall for an high King, an household to holden,
> With broad boards abouten, y- benched well clean,
> With windows of glass wrought as a church
> —*P. Ploughman's Crede* ii. 309

On the east side of the Cloister, next to the transept, was the

SACRISTY,

of which not a vestige remains, it was in this position at Thornton, Worksop, Oxford, Smithfield, and Hexham.

Happily, a very considerable portion of the

CHAPTER HOUSE

survives, now reduced to 47 ft. in length, and formerly 42 ft. in breadth, until the side walls were rebuilt and a trigonal apse added after the dissolution to form a room The fine central Portal consists of a large central entrance flanked by windows, as at Bristol It is of three orders, richly moulded and adorned with a flat four-leaved ornament and crowned heads as capitals, and terminals to the outer arch or label. On either side is an arch, that to the south has a peculiar three-leaved ornament; its fellow on the north is plain Each includes a window once divided by a mullion In the jambs of the arches are 14th century additions consisting of canopied saints, on the north are a mitred abbot with the staff in the left hand, and a primate holding his cross, perhaps S. Thomas of Canterbury; to the south stand S. Augustine mitred with the book of the Order and pastoral staff, and S Michael transfixing the old serpent. In the centre on the north are St. Catherine with her wheel and sword, and St. John Evangelist as on the conventual seal holding a pen, and with the other hand leading an eagle which bears a scroll inscribed with the first words of his Gospel. On the south again are S. John Baptist with the Holy Lamb, facing St. Margaret, who pierces the dragon with her cross-staff All stand on brackets carved with masks In the year 1813 these memorials of mediæval art had been subjected to coarse mutilation,

Chapter House, Haughmond Abbey.

From a Photograph by J. Laing, Shrewsbury.

and the whole site was uncared for. The oak ceiling is solid and massive, composed of strong moulded beams of the 14th century and deep panel work, divided by ribs. A flat string course completes the elevation, and also like the covering of the room points to the existence of an upper range forming the

<small>Gent Mag
lxxxiii 5, 39</small>

DORMITORY.

A small pointed doorway led to a Slype next the Chapter House, and a second door with some corbels near it opened into the calefactory or Common Hall of the Canons; both chamber and covered way being formed out of the undercroft of the upper dormitory. Between that building and the east wall of the Refectory, or below the place of the high table, another Slype led into a second or

BASE COURT,

which at Bristol, Oxford and Carlisle had the Infirmary upon the south side. On the east side of the quadrangle the ivied wall remains It has an arched doorway at the S E corner, adjoining a Pointed arch in the wall that here returns, and is continued westward to a junction with the southern range. This consists of two considerable buildings at right angles to each other. The easternmost runs north and south. It had formerly two gables, one crowned with a cross, the other pierced with a trefoil In the N.E. corner there is a well The pointed arch of the south end remains near an ancient window and a doorway, whilst in front of it there are remains of a large trigonal bay window in two tiers. Several square-headed windows and a fireplace were contemporaneous insertions of the 15th century.

<small>Add MS
27 765. F fo 9</small>

The next building running east and west has also been mutilated by the Barkers after the Suppression, and supplied with a mantle-piece with vignettes, roses, and festoons of ivy. It measures 81 × 36, and forms the most conspicuous feature of the abbey from the road, with its fine gable pierced with the casing of a Perpendicular window of four lights, and flanked by two stair turrets with conical cappings, The newel to the north contained a staircase which through a shouldered arch led to a passage in front of the west window (as at Bolton Priory), and on the south by a square-headed doorway opened upon a wall passage eastward At the N.E. angle again there is a doorway opening northward into the Base Court, and eastward into a stair turret with eleven steps, lighted by a quatrefoiled aperture and a square window The north side of this fine room retains only portions of its line of windows, but the sunshine is still admitted on the south through three graceful windows of two lights, trefoiled in the head, and formerly glazed, with a transom dividing the lower part, which was simply shuttered. A door on this side led into a garden, the wall of which and a southern entrance remain At the west end there is a large recessed double doorway, and on either side of it large doorways are pierced to communicate with an outer range of lateral passages, which formed part of the screens of this hall, the grooves for the partition on the east side still remain in the wall These buildings occupy the usual site of the

<small>Buck's View 1732</small>

INFIRMARY

<small>Duke's MS fo 243</small>

and the Infirmarer's Lodge Here the rooms communicate by two doors in the partition wall, which in 1731 retained its eastern gable. The two-light windows, trefoiled, with a trefoil in the head, are fine Decorated.

The west side of the Base Court connecting this Chamber and the Refectory, is filled up by the larder and the kitchen, which retains two huge external chimneys of the 14th century, and between them two square-headed windows and an earlier lancet The Claustral Prior had a chamber under the Dormitory, with an entry to the Cloister next the Parlour door, and a garden An unsavoury adjunct to the Great Gate was a stye for 80 hogs which supplied lard, first provided in 1332

ABBOTS OF HAGHMOND.

Eyton vii 282—

  Fulke, Prior,
  Ingenulf c. 1155-8
  Alured, tutor to K. Henry II c 1170
  William c 1176
  Richard c. 1180-1.
  John
  Ralph c. 1204-10
  Nicholas
  Osbert c, 1217-26
  William II. c. 1226.
  Ralph II
1236 —Hervey died 1241
  Engebrard.
1241.—Gilbert, Prior of Staines.
1253.—Alexander.
  John c. 1263
  Alan c. 1273-7
1280 —Dec. 4 —Henry de Astley
1304.—Gilbert de Campeden resigned.
  Richard de Broke. canon of Kenilworth, d 1325
  Nicholas de Longenore built the kitchen and confirmed Hugh
    Cheyne's Chantry in 1336
1346 —Robert de Brugge (Bridgnorth)

1348.—John.
    Richard.
    John de Smethcote.
    Nicholas Bircton c. 1377-80.
    Ralph c. 1386.
1415.—William,
    Roger Westley d. 1421.
1421.—Richard Burnell, resigned 1446.
1463.—John Ludlow, D.D., canon, confirmed the L'Estrange Chantry at S. Anne's Altar.
1495.—Richard Pontesbury,
1526.—Christopher.
    Thomas Corvesor surrendered with ten canons on Sept. 9, 1539. He had a pension of £40 a year. The net income of the Abbey was £294 12s. 9d.

The water system was once complete, and a most interesting

CONDUIT OR WELL HOUSE

remains on the bank above the Chapter House, embowered amongst trees, It is of the 14th century, measures 10 ft. 6 in, × 7 ft. 6 in. and has a gabled front, with a trefoiled niche for an image, and an opening to the fountain under a flattened arch head, The roof is formed of slabs of stone built in a steep slope from the side walls to the ridge.

The fish ponds were on the north side of the Church.

The deed of surrender on Sept. 9, 1541, now in the Public Record Office, has the seal attached to it representing S. John the Divine seated in a chair, with the eagle at his feet holding a scroll inscribed with the first words of his Gospel. A canon on either side offers his key of office. It has the legend S (igillum) Comune Capituli de Hagmon.

COPIED FROM BUCK'S VIEWS, 1731.

Haug

;MOND.

The following names are appended, the pensions I add from another source —

Thomas Abbot	...	£40	0	0
John Colfox, prior		£8	0	0
Sir Roger Mokyr (Mekyn)		£6	0	0
William Owen		£5	6	8
Hugh Cooke	...	£6	0	0
William Ryland		£6	0	0
William Rydge		£5	6	8
John Mathoos		£5	6	8
Thomas Lye (Lee)		£5	6	8
John Wright	...	£5	6	8
Thomas Clarke		£5	6	8

Augm off Misc. Books, 204 fo 90.

Two others did not sign, William Rolfe, who retired on £7, and Richard Doone on 40 shillings

The site, with belfry, church, and cemetery, was granted on Sept. 20. 1541, to Edward Littleton, of Pillaton Hall, Co Stafford, who sold it to Sir Rowland Hill, Knt, his sister and co-heir conveyed it to the Barkers their heiress brought it to the Kynastons from them it descended to the Corbets

Pa. Ro. 32 Henry VIII P iv m 12(35)

The Commission for taking the surrender was couched in the following words —

Henry VIII. to the right rev. father in God the Bpp of Chester, our right trustie and right well-beloved counsellor, and lorde president of our counsell in the Marches of Wales, and to our trustie and right well-beloved Sir Will Sulyarde, Knt, one of our Counseill there greeting. Forasmoche as we understand that the Monasterie of Hammond,* in our County of Salop,

*This is the phonetic spelling of the old form "Haeman" in a Charter of the time of Henry II —*Cartæ Harl.* iii c 29

F

remeanythe at the present in such state as the observance of the same, neither redundithe to the honour of God nor to the benefite of our Comonweal, We lat you wyt, that, therefore, beyng mynded to take the same into our owen handes for a better purpose, like, as we dubt not but that the Abbot and Convent of the same will be content to make their surrendre accordingly, We, for the special trust and confidence we have in yor approved fidelities, wisdomes, and discretiones, have, and by these presents do auctorise, name, assigne, and apoynte you, that immidiatly repairing to the said House shall receive of the hede and brether of the same such a writing undre their Convent seale as to yor discretions shall be thought mete and convenient for the due surrendre to our use of the same, and thereupon taking possession, and of all the goodes, catelle, plate, jewelles, implementes and stuffe, the leade and Bells excepted, to be indifferently solde eithe for redie money, or elles at dayes upon sufficient sureties. so that the same dayes passe not one yere and a halfe, ye shall delyver to the said Abbott and Convent such parte of the said moneye and goodes there for their despeche, and assigne unto the same such Pensions to be alleyvid out of the goods, landes, or revenues of the said House, as by yor wisdomes shall be thought mete and convenient

Which done, further seying, the rightfull and due debts there paid and satisfied as to reason and good conscience aperteynith, and yor owne chargis resonable allowing yorselves, ye shall procede to the Dissolution of the said House, and in our Name and behalf taking possession of the same and of all landes thereunto belonging or apperteynyne and delyver the custody of the said House Bells and leade to sum substanciall mete and convenient person salvely and surely to be kept to or use and profet

Ye shall, furthermore, bring and conveye to or Tower of London to the master of or Juelhouse there delyveryng unto hym by byll indented the reste of the money, plate, juelles and ornamentes that in anywise shall come to yor handes by means of the premises or of any part thereof

Stratly chardging and commanding all Mayors, sherefis, bailifes and constables, and all other or officers, ministers, and subjects to whome in this cace it shall apperteyn that unto you and every of you as they shall be by you required they be aiding, helping, and assisting as they will answer unto us for the contrary at their perilles

Geven undre or privie seale at our manor of Woodstock, the xxiij daye of Auguste in the xxxj yere of or reigne.

THOMAS CROMWELL,

The following answer was returned —

Omnibus Christi fidelibus ad quos præsens scriptum pervenerit Thomas, permissione divina abbas monasterii S Johannis Apostoli et Evangeliste de Haghmond in Com. Salopie, et ejusdem loci conventus salutem in Domino sempiternam Noveritis nos prefatos abbatem et Conventum, unanimis assensu et consensu, nostris animis deliberatis, certa scientia et mero motu nostris, ex quibusdam causis justis et racionabilibus nos animos et conscientias nostras spiritualiter moventibus, ultro et sponte dedisse et concessisse, ac per præsentes damus concedimus, reddimus, deliberamus, et confirmamus illustr. et invict principi et domino nostro, Henrico VIII°, Dei gratia etc, ac in terris supremo ecclesiæ Anglicanæ sub Christo capiti, totum dictum monasterium abbathiam sive domum nostram mansionem et ecclesiam de Haghmonde predictæ, ac totam scitum, fundum, circuitum, et precinctum ejusdem monasterii, necnon omnia et singula dominia, maneria, domos, messuagia, etc

Sept. 19, 1539   Signed by the abbot and 10 canons, Oct 16, 1539

It was a mere form which occurs also in the case of Lilleshall   The lesser houses were legally dissolved by Act of Parliament, now Henry and Cromwell extorted an illegal surrender, which had been preceded by the acknowledgment of the royal supremacy, and was followed only in the following reign by the reformation of religion   They were three distinct events, and virtually quite independent   Hitherto in previous reigns the revenues of religious houses which had been suppressed as alien or insignificant in size, were applied to similar purposes of godliness and useful learning   Now wanton desecration and unsparing sacrilege, and in some cases actual murder were committed to fill the purses of a tyrant and his courtiers

The last sight of the old inmates of the abbey occurs in 1553

Exch Q R
Misc Books
32, fo. xlviii

Haughmond 1553

	Rich. Bleke, liiis. vijd.
	Reginald Corbett, xxs.
Annuities and	Will Homer, xxs
Corrodies	Thos. Maynewaryng, cs
	Rich. Greyhorse, liijs. iiijd
	Rich. Lancashire, liiis. iiijd.
Pensions	Will. Regge, cvjs. viijd.
	Will Byland, vili
	Hugh Cooke, vili.
	Thos. Leigh, cvjs. viijd.

	Roger Mekyns, vi*li*
	John Mathew, cvj*s.* viii*d*
	Will Owen, cvj*s* viii*d*
	Christopher Keente, x*li*
Fees	Earl of Arundel, General Steward, xxvi*s* viij*d*
	Edward Lodge, Steward, vj*li* xiij*s*

It is a fact which redounds to the honour and repute of the Abbey that Sir Robert Grimbald, Justiciar of England, about the middle of the 12th century prescribed to his new foundation, Osulveston Priory, "the rule of Haughmond in Salop"

The Hospital of S. Mary, at Oswestry, founded by Bp Reiner, of S Asaph, was under the spiritual oversight of the Prior and Canons of Haughmond, who in 1210 undertook to maintain a chantry in its chapel, called Le Sputty ('Spital) and endowed with Wilcot manor   Eyton, x, 345

A seal of Haughmond is in the British Museum marked iii c 29

The Particulars for Grants in the Public Record Office, unfortunately, are very meagre in regard to the Shropshire Monasteries   In allotting these buildings, therefore, I have been guided by the minute account of Oseney Abbey, which Antony A' Wood collected not only from charters and ruins, but also by direct tradition   A single additional touch would mar the graphic symplicity and vivid description of a sympathising eye-witness who could make the whole scene arise from the dust and live again

"The footway led to the first and least of the gates and then came to the   Wood MS.

<small>Bodl. Libr.
Oxf. F. 29.
ff. 215-216
b.</small>

GREAT GATE, adjoining thereto was a little cabin or cell for the janitor to lodge in, who, according to the Rule, was to be "probabilis vitæ, senex et sapiens" His office was to keep the gates for the most part shut, not to let any in without leave from the abbot, to have an eye towards the young canons in their wandering to and fro, to keep out lay people and young women, especially men bearing weapons or suspicious varlets who not only come with an intent to filch, but also to pry into the actions of the canons, and so thereby take advantage to slander though falsely their conversation and render them odious to the vulgar He was also to receive poor people and pilgrims with love and in the name of God, not to let them abide long at the gate to the disturbance of the quiet, but send them away with refreshment, for which purpose he had several loaves appointed by the cellarer, to be laid in his cell to distribute to them, especially on fasting days, when there was no offal meat from the refectory So great it seems was their care in relieving all sorts of people that pretended poverty, that though corn was often scarce by reason of famines that happened in those days, yet rather than send them away empty would diminish their usual allowance at times of refection to relieve them.

"After the entrance into the Great Gate, which was on the north side of the abbey, was beheld a spacious Court or quadrangle, for the most part of freestone, and situated at the west end of the church from the Gate on the left hand, and so all under the said end of the church was a spacious cloister decked and beautified with a boarded roof, having the arms of benefactors thereon, as also several rebuses and allusions intimating those persons

"Going through the cloister the passenger was conducted to the Refectory, a Common Hall, which was of a large and curious structure on the south side of the quadrangle It was the common place of resort where all did meet at the sound of the bell to take their diet, for the manner and decency that they used in eating was that according to their Rule the Scripture should be read and expounded that so their souls as well as their bodies might the same time be fed with spiritual food; that no contentions or quarrelsome words fall out between them, that at the blessing of the table all appear in presence, and if any absent then to lose his portion of meat for that time and sit at the lower end of the table, and lastly, whatever was left of their meat was conveyed to the almshouses or Domus Dei, adjoining to the Abbey. Their meat was served from the kitchen adjoining to the Refectory on the west side, both ample and convenient for the purpose, where for their accommodation they had a Cistern that stood in the middle of the Court, and that also supplied by an aqueduct.

" Behind the Refectory on the south side was the nosocomium or Infirmary or the Firmary, which was a place allotted purposely for the sick canons when they were removed from their chambers, and where they had all things convenient according to their condition, both for matter of diet foreseen by the cellarer, as also a physician and an overseer or attendant who was called Infirmarer. Adjoining to it was a little chapel or oratory where there were prayers said (for ?) to them by one of the officers of the church every day

" The next place observable is the Dormitory or Dortor It was a long room divided in several partitions In every one was a bed resembling much those long chambers at Eton and Winchester, used for the same purpose by the children there In this Dortor all the canons except those that were aged, infirm, or employed with offices belonging to the abbey slept Every one had his bed to himself, and that also open at the feet towards the common passage that the præfect as he went by might see whether each kept his place after every one of them was reposed. There was a candle set up to burn for the most part of the night, or in case any canons should fall sick, or at least to serve till the time of performing their Nocturns or prayers appointed for certain hours of the night The candle being lighted, the keys of the Dortor were carried to the præfect or vicar by the servitour belonging thereto, and by him again at the appointed hour in the morn opened, then each canon receiving their summons to rise had half an hour or thereabouts allowed them both in making up themselves and their beds

" To pass by the particular lodgings of the canons adjoining to the river we come to the ABBOT'S LODGINGS without the Common Court or quadrangle, they were very spacious, fair, and large, and had a hall more befitting a common society than a private man Herein the abbot and his family (household) and sometimes tenants and strangers of quality did for the most part take his refection, excepting some particular high days, when his presence was required in the public Refectory Great stone steps led up to the Hall.

"There was a row of building at the entrance between the two gates and joining to the way leading to the Abbey Gate, it was called GOD'S HOUSE, and allotted for poor clerks and other indigent people servile about the abbey and that lived with the offall meat that came from the canons' table and a maintenance or liveries They had a chapel joining to their habitation

"Chiefly bound to their cloister they did both to exercise their bodies and devotion, and make the tediousness of their life seem more pleasant, expend much in finishing of pleasant walks by the river side, and environing them with elm trees, as also orchards, and arbours that were divided with cunning meanders, as fishponds, dovecots and what not, situated on the south side of their buildings" Thus far I have used the words of Wood

THE DRESS AND RULE OF AUSTIN CANONS.

I may add that the habit of an Austin canon was a linen rochet, a black cope, a hat, and round-toed boots, a compromise between the habit of a secular canon and a monk.

The injunctions of bishops to houses of the order, which, unlike those of monks, were subject to episcopal visitation, give us a lively picture of the internal life of the canons They conversed in Latin In the cloister they read in their carols or studies, or else sat absorbed in silent contemplation with their hoods drawn over their eyes In the Dormitory a light burned all through the night, the beds were fixtures, without foot curtains, at a signal from the refectory bell the community after compline entered two and two. Strict silence was kept, and no pet birds, such as ravens and doves, were permitted. Before dinner the canons washed at the lavatory, and the prior when he took his seat rang his bell, and said Benedicite. During dinner the reader for the week read aloud from the Holy Bible or some religious book, and at the conclusion of the meal the canons went to church singing the Miserere in procession. The laundryman brought home the clean clothes on Saturday. In summer, after the Gracias in choir, the convent was allowed to sleep for half an hour in the Dormitory, and then say Nones, after which they washed their hands and studied in cloister, except on days of recreation (Tuesday and Thursday) No canon was to go abroad without a companion. At the beginning of the 15th century they laid aside the use of boots, such as monks used, and adopted shoes and socks

The great Benedictine abbeys claimed exemption from diocesan jurisdiction, the Cistercian paid fealty to the parent houses in France, and the

Cluniacs turned to Clugny or La Charité, paying the penalty of aliens by the levy of heavy fines to the English crown, if there was time to escape wholesale confiscation. The regular canon on the other hand was subject in extreme cases to visitation by the bishop of the diocese. Thus, in 1329, Bishop Roger of Lichfield ordered silence to be observed at Haughmond at proper hours in Church, Refectory, Dormitory, and Cloister, the removal of hounds for the chace, and of Alice and Agnes Goodwyn from the outer precincts, forbidding also rash gifts of corrodies, sale of pensions or donations of coal to the foresters. The brewer and hostillar were removed. A proper person was appointed to collect the fragments for the poor at the Abbot's hall door, and the porter was to deliver them daily at dinner time. The decree was to be read yearly on Ash Wednesday in full chapter. Discipline had clearly been neglected, but the abbot was worn down with the burden of long years and sickness, and his canons accused him of manumitting natives, destroying the woods, and contracting debts, but they had no complaint of two of their number who preferred to pass their time in the freedom of Blaford Grange until the bishop summarily recalled them.

I have been able to find only one reference to the spoil of Haughmond and its treasury, but it is valuable as a proof that it was a mitred abbey, a fact hitherto unknown.

<small>Monastic Treasures 20</small>

"The Bishop of Chester, by thandes of Edwarde Williams, delivered from the late monasterye of Hagmonde, in the Countie of Saloppe, a mytour, the grounde white silke, garnished with silver and gilte counterfete stones and small seede perles, lacking parte of the garnishinge, and a crosier staffe of woode and iron, the garnishing thereof silver and the crosse silver, poz. lxiii oz. as by an indenture of the xxth of November, anno xxxmo, over and besides x£ xiiijs. iijd. received in money and charged after in this accompte in the title of redy money."

Lilleshull Abbey. Western Doorway.

From a Photograph by J. Laing, Shrewsbury

THE AUSTIN CANONS' ABBEY

OF

S. MARY,

IN LILLESHULL WOOD.

---✠---

"In which they had vowed all
"Their life to service of high heaven's King:
"Did spend their lives in doing godly thing:
"Their gates to all were open evermore,
"That by the weary way were travelling."—Spenser.

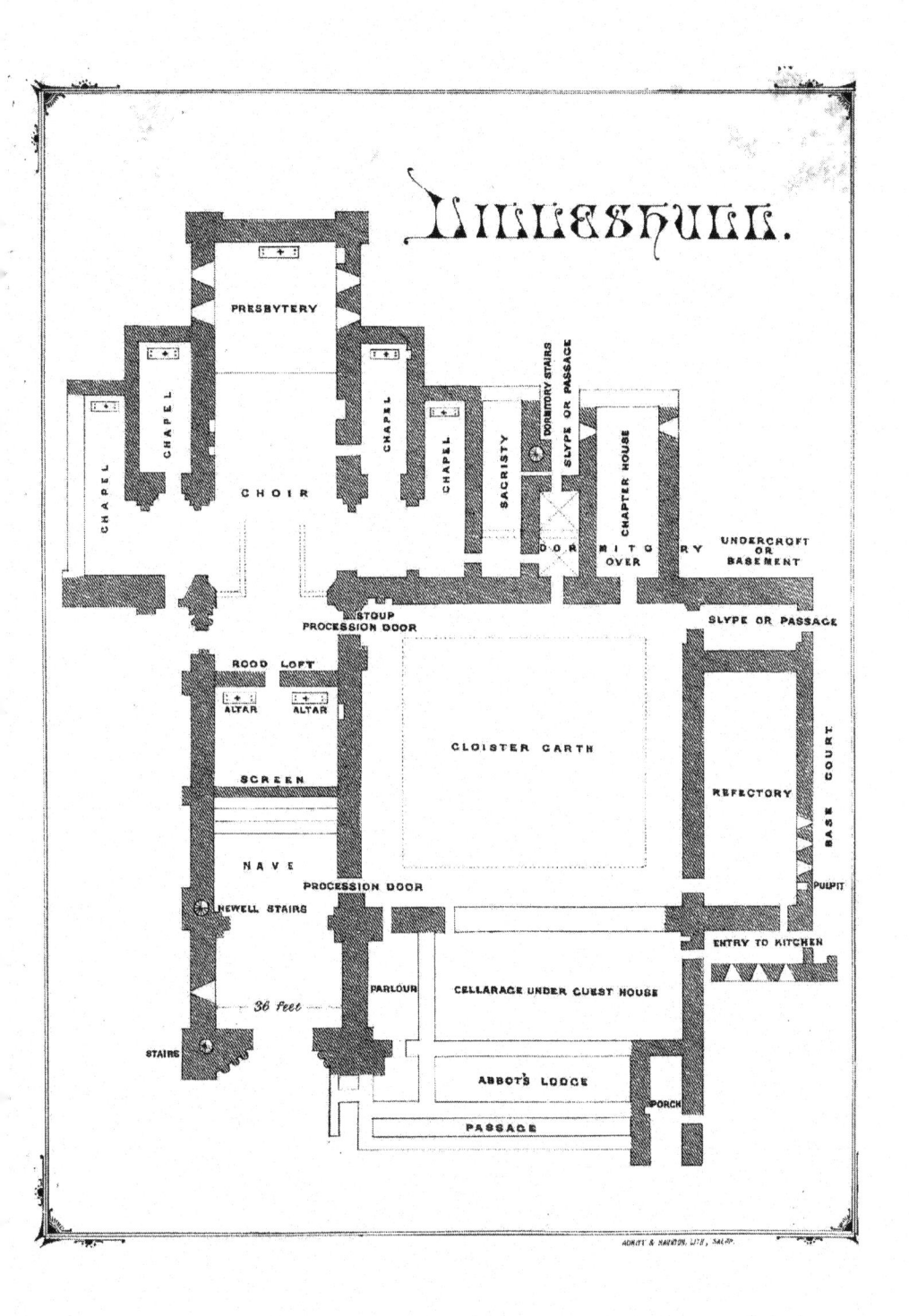

LILLESHULL.

St. Mary's Abbey, in the Wood of Lilleshull.

THE name of Lilla is familiar to the readers of Bede as that borne by the chivalrous and devoted servant of Edwyn King of Northumbria, who interposed his body as a buckler between his master's heart and the poisoned dagger of an assassin. Lilla's Hill must commemmorate, therefore, some early Saxon lord of the domain. Among all the abbeys of the Austin Canons there is none which exceeds in interest Lilleshull. The minster has many peculiar features, and the conventual buildings are almost complete, and compare to advantage with the smaller portions left at S. Andrew's, N.B., Oxford, Bristol, Carlisle, Hexham, and Lanercost.

Hist Eccl lib II, c IX, Comp Lilleshain Kemble's Cod Dipl (854) n. Mliu.

FOUNDATION OF THE ABBEY

According to the charter "Canons of Arroasia," (S. Nicholas, Arras,) from S Peter's Church, at Dorchester, came to build the Abbey of S. Mary ever Virgin in Lilleshall Wood." They were a branch of the great Order of S. Augustine, and had houses at Cambuskenneth, Harewold, Hartland,

Harl. MS 3868 ff 22-24

Brunne and Nutley. Alexander the Magnificent, bishop of Lincoln, had given them a home at Dorchester in 1140. The Oxfordshire Canons, although they did not reproduce the ground plan of their own ill-shaped minster, built here exceptionally a church without aisles Archdeacon Richard de Beaumes, the founder, placed them at first on Lizard Grange, near Tong, and in 1144, being then prebendary, as afterwards he was dean of S. Alkmund's, Shrewsbury, transferred them to Donnington Wood, six miles distant, on his prebendal grange, which was granted to him by the King , and thence they removed three miles further to Lilleshull, about the year 1148 His brother Philip, lord of Tong, and nephew of Richard, bishop of London, who had introduced practically the Regular Canons of St. Austin constituted as a distinct order by the Lateran Council in 1133, followed out his uncle's plan, and divided his interest between them and the Cistercian abbey of Buildwas Hence they settled primarily upon his estates In 1145 K. Stephen granted all the remaining prebends as they fell vacant to the new foundation

Few sites can compete with Lilleshull, and though the ruined roofless masses of grey stone conflict with the fresh green of the leaves, and undecorated walls cannot harmonize with the smooth verdant carpet that tapestries the floor, we may wonder how it is that here the builders did not drink in inspiration from the avenues of forest trees, the interlacing boughs above their heads, and the rich foliage, the fern and the chestnut, the lily and the rose to deck niche and capital They studied not when the golden sunlight and autumn tints flush with glorious stains the woodland depths, but rather when the breath of winter has stripped them of their bravery. In the loveliest spot a path of aisleless walls now leads up to a group of chapels, and we miss the stately nave and misty alleys, forming the grand approach to a noble east-end. The interior, measuring 225 ft × 31 ft., is confused in plan, narrow at one end, and

<small>Memoir by E Jones 1865, and B r i t Arch Assoc. Jo xv 265</small>

Lilleshull Abbey from S.W.

From a Photo. by J. Laing, Shrewsbury.

then branching out into many deep alleys, confined here by screens and side altars, and there multiplied into divergent parts It must have failed in giving that impression of infinity made visible, which the more perfect ground plans of complete minsters were designed to convey. Still we may be thankful that whilst so little remains of the grander foundations of Guisborough and Kirkham, or Clugniac Lewes, and when the glories of S Edmund's Bury, Reading, Hyde, St. Augustine's Canterbury, Battle, Coventry, Hulme, Evesham and Glastonbury not inferior to the Benedictine churches which survive, and the noble Cistercian shrines of Waverley, Ford, Beaulieu, Boxley, Robertsbridge, Louth Park, Quarr and Jorevalle have faded as a dream, we still retain a relic which preserves so much of its ancient condition.

The nearest station is at Donnington, two miles distant, and the road lies through the model village with its trim-built houses, and then we diverge to the right between a farm house and standing water, along a pleasant country way, woody and sequestered for a mile, until we turn in by a gate on the left over a green plot of sward, into the shady quiet nook belted with trees.

THE WEST FRONT.

We see before us the mutilated abbey front. It has a noble portal, c, 1190-1200, round-headed, of three orders, with a four-leaved flower in the outer moulding , the shafts have been destroyed, but one capital of great beauty in form and foliage remains On the outer abaci there were seated figures. On the south was a stair turret, retaining its door, and on the north another with a newel, large and broad, has an upper arcading of three arches with trefoiled heads According to tradition there was a Perpendicular super-

Duke's MS.
Bodl Lib
fo. 327.

structure (as at Benedictine Malmesbury, Leominster, and Shrewsbury,) forming a tower. At Waltham and Christchurch Hants, Dorchester and Oseney, (as in the Cistercian Whalley and Furness,) there was also a west tower In the interior vaulting-shafts and the door of the N.E. newel staircase remain.

THE NAVE.

In the centre of the nave there are three steps leading up to the basement of a screen which probably divided off the parish church until in 1285, on March 6, a separate vicarage of St Michael with its manse altarage and mortuary was allowed by the bishop. A second division may have been occupied by the servants and infirm canons. At the east end there was a rood screen, with a central doorway, flanked by two altars, " enclosed with oak," of which the base courses and a double drain on the south (its conventional) side remain These partitions throw light on the arrangement of Haughmond nave and its graduated bays. Two Processsional doorways are pierced through the south wall, which is 45 feet high, and, apparently, had no windows, whilst at the upper end of the north side there is a noble Pointed window with tripled nook shafts, over a very fine doorway of similar design which led to the Cemetery Tiles of six patterns have been exhumed, one represents a tree torn up by its roots, a fatal symbolism prophetical of the wreck in which it was found buried

A third screen was erected at the entrance of the Ritual choir, which occupied the crossing, and the two next bays eastward. The space between this parclose and the rood screen with its lateral doors, formed the ante-choir or conventual nave The western arch has the terminals of the vaulting shafts, like those in the choir, corbelled off to admit the canopies of the stalls, and their basement can still be traced. The shafts are tripled, and have square abaci and scolloped capitals. The STALLS, sixteen in number, are said to have been removed to the Collegiate Church of S Peter, Wolverhampton, in 1544, by Sir Walter Leveson, and are now shown in the Great Chancel.

Oliver's Wolverhampton, p 61

THE TRANSEPT.

The Transept is less perfect than the nave The south wing retains the door to the Sacristy, and on the east two round-headed arches stript of their ashlar, large and of equal size, which opened into two parallel chapels. Portions of the east and south walls of the northern and larger chapel remain. It has in the S.E. angle a small square-headed aumbry, and a drain corbelled out.

The north wing was of the same design. One round arch opens into the eastern chapel, a pointed arch on the west, and a few crumbling walls remain. This arrangement of double chapels of great size may be seen at Oxford, and a single one, the Elder Lady Chapel at Bristol, on the north side, but the more exact parallel occurs in the long flanking chapels, one on either side of the Presbytery of Llanthony, and the parish church of St Mary, Shrewsbury, and in the Benedictine Priory of S. John, Brecon. The Chapels were dedicated to the Blessed Virgin on the north side, which had its own organs and screen; S. Michael, newly built before the suppression; and S. Anne, with three altars.

THE RITUAL CHOIR.

The eastern arm and transept are Late or Transitional Norman. The eastern arm was divided into two parts, the two westernmost bays formed a portion of the Ritual choir, and the two eastern constituted the Sanctuary. In the CHOIR a door opens into the south chapel, near a round-headed sepulchral recess, with dwarf pillars of early English date, to receive an effigy. In the north wall there are two monumental recesses.

THE PRESBYTERY

The PRESBYTERY was lighted by two windows in the lower tier, and four round-headed windows on either side forming the clerestory. It had a large five-light east window of the beginning of the 15th century, which retained part of its tracery in 1829 Its case, like the recess for the Sedilia, only remains now There was no triforium throughout the building as in the Cistercian churches of Kirkstall and Buildwas

THE SACRISTY.

The Sacristy intervenes between the Transept and the Slype, and has a barrel vault divided by a stone beam A door formed a communication with the south wing of the church, and another facing it led into the Slype. In the south-east angle there is a projecting newel staircase which formed the approach at night from the Dormitory above.

CONVENTUAL BUILDINGS.

The CLOISTER GARTH is almost surrounded by its ancient buildings. On the east side a single round-headed deeply splayed window above the

SLYPE indicates what was once a noble series of windows lighting the DORMITORY which formed a continuous superstructure on this side.

The eastern PROCESSION DOOR is finely designed It is of five orders, the arches and mouldings have chevrons and a diamond-fretty pattern enclosing balls. The capitals are carved with rude foliage, and two of the shafts are channelled, whilst two more have the diamond-fretty and zig-zag ornaments, reversed ; the inner arch has an angle-head, and little circles in lozenges within the tympanum Adjoining it is the holy water stoup used on entering or leaving the church Further to the south, under a chevroned arch, are aumbries for books used in the time of cloister reading, to which the north aisle was invariably assigned

EAST SIDE OF THE CLOISTER SQUARE

Passing the fine doorway of the SLYPE, which had quadripartite vaulting in two spans and an eastern outlet, we see the bases of the doorway of the Chapter House, and miss a splendid ornament of the alley. It was of three orders, the voussoirs were wedge shaped, the pilaster shafts were on the outer sides carved with the scale pattern, and the capitals of the rest had the pellet ornament above foliage ; the inner arch had an indented moulding. The chamber itself was an oblong, and where the walls clear the lateral buildings, there is a round-headed window on either side of the east end A string course is carried along the blank walls which, as at Haughmond, were covered with a flat ceiling There is a sepulchral slab with a floriated cross upon the floor, possibly that of Lady Hillary de Tressebut, who desired to be laid here to her rest. This side of the Garth was completed by the undercroft of the Dormitory.

Duke's MS
fo 327
Buck's View,
1732

THE SOUTH SIDE OF THE CLOISTER SQUARE.

The southern line has two doorways facing the Procession-doors of the Church The eastern one is the approach to a Slype or passage, continued parallel with the wall of the refectory, and opening on the south side into the Base Court of the Infirmary. The western door, which is round-headed in two courses of masonry, with its sub-arch like the entrance to the Slype, opened into the REFECTORY This grand hall occupied almost the entire length of the garth or square, and had towards it a pent roof carried upon corbels, one of which is in place The south wall retains three lofty round-headed windows, and a pulpit with a quatrefoil pierced in the rear wall and a round arch above, in which the voussoirs resemble shields suspended by a cord To the east of it is a deep recess or dresser under a flattened arch A miserable modern wall bisects this room, which appears utterly neglected amid the general care bestowed upon the ruins A square-headed door in the west wall forms the entrance from a passage between the kitchen on the south and the cellarage on the north On the west side of this ENTRY TO THE KITCHEN there is a trefoiled light between two large round-headed windows A fire-place remains near the outer or south door, and possibly marks the Calefactory or chamber for warmth, and a fourth door occurs in the south-west angle

THE WEST SIDE OF THE CLOISTER SQUARE.

The west side of the Garth as at Bolton, Lanercost, Smithfield, S Andrew's N.B , Hexham, Walsingham, and Worksop was formed by CELLAR-AGE, with probably the Abbot's gallery, chapel, and hall (as at S. Osyth's) ; and the Guest house in a parallel line exterior to it, except at the northern end, where there are remains of the Forensic or OUTER PARLOUR for conversation with strangers and visitors, indicated by walls to the west, and on the east by a door which immediately adjoins the jambs of the western Procession-door. A second door led from the Cellarage, which seems from a corbel head in the wall to have been vaulted in two spans At Lanercost the Abbot's Lodge is on the S.W. of the church and the cellarage on the west of the cloister

At the S.W. corner of the enclosure or precinct there are some portions of parallel walls with a square-headed window and a door in the southern fragment which faces a recess in the opposite block of masonry. This probably formed a porch to the Gate House with a porter's lodge.

The arrangements of the Fratry, Dortor, and Chapter House were the same at Bridlington as here detailed in two documents now in the Public Record Office A Prior's Lodge occupied the west side of the Cloister, the " Long House of Office" or Gong communicated on the S W. with the Dormitory, which the "treasury house" in a tower adjoined. On the east side of the Dormitory were the " Fermory " with its chapel; the new chamber, and the high cellarer's chamber. The lodgings for strangers adjoined the Gate House Lord Bacon in the Atlantis has provided us with a striking picture of the " Strangers' House, with handsome and cheerful chambers, the Long Gallery, like a Dorture, with cells having partitions of wood, all along one side, instituted as an Infirmary for sick persons " For awhile the grantees, partly under the first terms of tenure, in order to soften the loss of Guest House and poor men's lodging, occupied some of the buildings, then the country folk grew in time accustomed to the absence of conventual hospitality, and the houses were left to fall into ruin, so that if we wonder at the self-sacrifice of the founders raising magnificent structures far away from the abodes of men, we marvel more that there should have been found persons of education capable of destroying or leaving them to wreck, or Christians ready to do the work befitting a heathen mob or creedless conqueror

The seal of the Abbey in the Public Record Office represents the Blessed Virgin holding a lily sceptre and the Holy Child. Ave is inscribed at her side, and the legend is *Sigillum ecclesie Beate Marie de Lilleshull*, the name in Domesday is spelt Linleshelle

<small>Lyton viii 210 Harl MS 2060 f 54. 8, 3868 fo 295 Add. MS 6155.</small>

The abbey had many benefactors John L'Estrange gave the Church of S Mary, Hulme-by-the-Sea, Co Norfolk All Saints', North Molton, S Helen's, Esseby (Ashby-de-la-Zouch), and S Margaret's Chapel, Blackfordeby, were given by Alan-de-la-Zouch St Michael's, Badminton, was added in 1370; and Farnborough, Co. Warwick, in 1345. Attingham, S Michael's, Lilleshull, and S. Alkmund's, Shrewsbury, were appropriated at an early date, and at various times Longdon and St Edmund's with the chapelry of Barwile.

<small>Blakeway's MS Bodl Lib fo 352</small>

A few details of inner life have been preserved. On Maunday Thursday they distributed 40s, and on September 8th, 4s in memory of the founder. When Roger Norreis the abbot died in the reign of Edward III. a bead roll was sent round to all the Confederated Monasteries which interchanged offices of devotion in this form.—

"Titulus" (the name of the convent is inserted) "pro animâ dompni Rogeri abbatis de Lilleshull. Animæ omnium defunctorum per misericordiam Dei in pace requiescant Vestris nostra damus pro nostris vestra rogamus" It was found in the Bodleian Library.

In 1468 the abbot agreed to celebrate a daily mass for Heywood dean and benefactor of Lichfield Cathedral, the chaplain receiving 6d. a week and on his obit the pitanciar or bursar of bequests paid to the abbot 20d, and half that sum to each canon who was present The Priest of Jesus Chantry at Lichfield also received a yearly fee of £6 13s 4d

Abbots who received the joint assent of the crown and diocesan — *Eyton VIII 212 -.*

    1148 —William died c 1174 *see Sarum Charters, Rolls S 97 p. 15*
        Walter died c. 1203
        Ralph c 1216.
        Alan
May 4, 1226 —William de Derleng
Aug. 9, 1235 —Simon de Fodering (Fotheringay).
Dec 14, 1240 —Richard de Salop, canon.
June 15, 1253.—Robert de Arkalaw.
Nov. 30, 1270 —William de Hales, prior.
        Luke, c. 1277-82 *Eyton ix 380*
        Ralph c. 1284-9.
        John
    Nov. 1291.—William de Bruge resigned Feb 28, 1308
    1308 —John de Chetwynd, canon
        Henry de Stokes, c. 1330
Aug. 6, 1350 —Robert de Ashby, canon
        William de Peplow, died 1369
        Roger Norreis, c. 1371.
        William de Peyntone c. 1376-92.
        William Lye, canon, c. 1400-28.
        John de Wenlock, c. 1431-63.
    1465.—Robert Fitz-John.
        Geoffrey Barton, c. 1498-1516 ⎫ *SCP V 70*
        James Cockerell, c 1518-20 ⎭

Robert Watson resigned Oct. 16, 1538, to Dr. Lee, who visited Shrewsbury for the surrender on Jan 24, Wenlock on Jan. 26, 1539-40, and Haughmond on Sept 9, 1539

Rymer vi, P 3, pp 43 46

With the Abbot the following canons were driven out —

John Hall, prior.
Christopher le Dyes
Thomas Dasun
John Rolles sub-prior
Roger Gnosaller
Thomas Maynard, cellarer.
William Massey
Peter Robinson.
Richard Cuerton
William Styche

Deed of Surrender Publ Rec Off, Blakeway MS ff 354, 359

The income of the abbey was £229 1s 3½d by the year.

The site by Henry VIII with that of Wombridge Priory was granted first to William Cavendish, and then on Dec 24, 1539, to James Leveson, from whom it has descended to the Duke of Sutherland, with its mines of untold wealth so long lying secret beneath the surface of the the manors, and now producing the revenue of princes.

A curious and valuable survey—a document of the greatest rarity—fortunately gives us a very complete insight into the condition of the Minster and Conventual buildings at the time of the Dissolution.

Augm. Off Books 172, fo. 21

" Hereafter folowyth all suche parcells of implements or household stuffe corne, catell, ornaments of the Churche, and such other like founde wythin the late monastery ther at the tyme of the dissolucon of the same house, solde by

COPIED FROM BUCK'S VIEWS, 1731

ESHULL.

the kyngs Commissionors unto Mr. Willm Cavendyssh, esquier, as particularly and plainly folowyth :—

The CHURCHE.—An Alter of woode paynted at the hyghe Altar; iiij candlestyks of brasse and ij litell candlestyks; the deskes in the Church; the Chapell of Saynt Michell, new made by the abbott; iij lytel altars in the Chapell of St Anne, a lytell payre of organes, an altar in our Lady Chapell and ij images, a partycon (particion) and seates of oke; the pavements in our Lady Chapel, a payr of organs in our Lady Chappell; the pavying in the body of the Church; in the body of the Church ij altars inclosed with oke; the rood-loft . .   lxs

The VESTRYE.—xi copes of olde bleue baudkyn, (from Baldacca Bagdad · tissue or cloth of gold, with figures embroidered in silk), iij copis of whyte baudkyn, iij other copis of whyte counterfeit baudekyn; viij olde copis of dyverse sorts, vi olde copis of dornyx, (rich stuff from Doornix or Tournay), a sewte of bleue baudkyn; another sewte of bleue baudkyn, a sute of redde sylke full of armes, viij old alter clothys, ij alter clothes to hange before alters   .   ,   ixs

THE FRATER.—v tables ther sould for . . ijs

THE CLOYSTER.—The laver (conduit), the cloyster rofe, schingle, (laths or thin wooden tiles to cover roofs), and paving stones. In the Chapter House the glasse wyndowe, ieron, and the paving stones, and the selles (little rooms partitioned off) in the Dorter (Dormitory), are soulde for . . iijli

THE HALLE.—ij tables; ij formes; j longe benche joyned (of joyners' work or wainscot), and an olde cobbord sould for xijd

THE PERLORE.—j taball; iij chayres; i forme and olde paynted clothes, (linen clothes painted with devices to hang on walls) xijd.

I

The Buttery —vij ale tobbes; j olde cobborde, vij table clothes; viij napkyns; ij towells, ij basons: ij euers; ij candalstykes; ij chyppyng (cutting up) knyves. . . xs.

Dorrell's Chamber —j bedstede, ij formes, j fetherbedd; j boulster; j pyllowe, j matres, ij blanketts, j coverlett; j olde tester (upper part of a bed) paynted, j olde hangyng (curtain), ij cherys; i lytell oulde table; ij cousshyons soulde for. iijs iiijd.

The Inner Chamber —ij fether beddes; ij boulsters; ij matres; j blankett, and ij coverletts soulde for vjs.

The Long Chamber —ij bedstedes, ij matrysys, ij coverletts, and i lytell oulde boulster soulde for xxd.

The Chamber at the Halle Door —j bedsted, j fether bedd; j boulster; j coverlett; and j matres soulde for ijs

The Newe Lodgeing.—iij fether bedes; iij coverletts, iij blanketts, iij boulsters, iij lytell stolys, j lytell shorte table, j oulde tester, estemyd to be worth . . xs.

The Knyghte's Lodgeyng —ij bedstedes; ij fether bedes; ij boulsters, ij coverletts, ij blanketts, j chayre; j olde table, and j olde paynted clothe sould for . . xs

The Seconde Chamber in Knyghte's Lodgeyng —ij bedstedes, ij formes, ij fetherbedes; ij boulsters, ij pyllowes; ij coverletts; ij blanketts; ij pyllowes; ij coverlets; ij blanketts, and olde paynted clothes . . vjs.

The Third Chamber in the same Lodgeyng.—ij fether bedes; ij boulsters; ij blankets, ij coverletts, and j paynted cloth. . . . iijs. iiijd.

THE CHAMBER WITHIN THE HALLE DORE.—ij lytell fether bedes; ij coverlettes; and ij boulsters soulde for ijs. iiijd.

THE KECHYNNE.—vi brasse pottes; iiij pannes, iiij spyttes; ij frying panne, j payr of rostyting ierounes; j barre to hang pots on; iij potthokes; j morter (a vessell for pounding) of brasse, j garneyshe and di (a set and a half) of pewter vessell sould to   Willm. Cavendysh, Esquier, for xls.

THE BREWEHOUSE —j leade, j panne of brasse, broken in the bottomme; j fatt of woode; xj colying leades (coolers); j brasse panne, j yelyng fatte, (vat for brewing ale), and iiij tubbes sold for iiijli

THE BAKEHOUSE—iij troughes, j boultyn hutche (a vessel for sifting meal); j mouldyng borde; (for making dough into loaves); and j bushell sould for xijd

THE DAYRY HOUSE —j olde table, j forme; iij lytell olde brasse pottes, j olde panne, j skylett (a small vessel with feet for boiling), certein oulde tobbes of lytell valure, iij shelfe bordes; ij bedstedes in the chamber, ij matressys; ij boulsters; ij coverletts; ij blanketts ij payr of shettes, and xi cheses . . . . vs.

HAYE SOULDE —Found ther xxx lodes at ijs. the lode, wych amountyth to the some of lxs

CATTELL.—xviij oxen there at xiijs iiijd the pece, one with another xijli. Mylch Kyne xv, and j bull xs. the pece, wych amountyth to the some of viijli.

    xx yonge steres and heffors at vjs the pece . vili.
    viij young wenyng calves at ijs the pece . . xvjs.
    xi shepe and lambes at xijd. the pece . . . . . xis.
    x kynne and a bull at Lupsty Parke prised at vjs. viijd. the pece .
lxxiijs. iiijd.   Total xxxijli ixs. iiijd.

GRAYNE SOULD.—Whete, by estimacyon j quarter sould for viijs.
RYE—xiij quarters at vjs viijd . . . iiijli xiijs. iijd.
BARLEY.—xx quarters at iiijs le quarter . . iiijli.
OTES.—x quarters at ijs. viijd le quarter . . xxvjs viijd
DREGE (Oats and Barley mixed)—x quarters at iijs the quarter . . .
xxxs. Total xjli. xviijs

Waynes, Ploues, with other thynges necessary to theme belongyng, iij waynes, with themes and other thyngys necessary belongyng unto them, iij ploues; and ij harrowes sould for xxxijs

Swyne . . xxv. hogges xxxs.

GYLTE PLATE SOULD —Plate soulde to George Warren, which was upon a boke, and j olde crosse staffe wayng xxv. ounces, at iiijs the ounce, which amountyth to the sume of ciiijs

The summe totall of all the guddes founde within the seid late Monastery, with ciiijs for xxvj ounces of gilte plate . . lxxiiijli xviijs.

Rewards given to the Chanons of the seid late Monastery.—To

Sir John Hall	...	1s.	Sir William Stutche	...	1s
Sir Christopher Ledis		1s	Sir Richard Cureton		1s
Sir Thomas Dawson		1s	Sir Thomas Maynard	...	1s.
Sir John Ponsebury		1s	Sir Peter Robinson	.	lvs.
Sir Roger Knowsall		1s.	Sir William Masye	. .	xis.
			Totall ..	..	xxvli

Rewardes given to the Servauntes of the seid late Monastery in lykewise at ther departure (there are 43 recipients of sums varying from 3s 4d to 26s. 8d, including the Scolemaster, xxvjs viijd · Willm Lakyng, gent. xxs., Thomas Brueiton, gent. xvs., William Sandrobe, gent. xxs.; the convent launder (laundryman) iijs ; ij plumbers iijs iiijd.; iiij gentylmen's sones xiijs iiid. Total xxviijli xvs. iiijd

For cates bought and spente at the tyme of the Commissionors beying there for dissolucion of the seid late Monastery and for the safe kepyng of the guddes and catell of the same during the seid tyme. . . . viij*li.* xvs. vj*d.* Money payd beforehande to Sir Thomas Layton, chauntery preste at Lychefeld, for hys halfe yere's pencion to hym, due at the feast of All Saynts, next before the date underwritten, viz, the xvii day of October, in the xxx yere of the reigne of our sovereigne lorde Kyng Henry the viijth, in consideracion of hys debilte and syknes lxvjs. viij*d* The summe of the payments aforeseid is lxv*li.* xvijs vj*d*, and so remayneth over ix*li.* vi*d* Certein guddes of stuffe appertaynyng to the seid Monastery remayneth unsolde.

GYLTE PLATE UNSOLDE.—iiij chalesys and ij stondyng cuppes, with one kyver all gylte, weing lxiij oz.

WHYTE PLATE UNSOLDE.—j sencer, j broken crosse staffe, j crosse of sylver; xj spones, ij saltes wythoute covers, all white, weing iiij xvi *oz*

BELLES REMAYNYNG UNSOLDE.—Ther remayneth vij belles weing xxxvij, and not as yete soulde, but valued at lxvj*li* xjijs. iiij*d.*

LEADE REMAYNYNG UNSOLD.—Ther remaynyth in leade c fothers at iiij*li* le fother; in the hole cccc*li*

MD.—Ther remayneth all the housys edifyed upon the scite of the seid late Monastery, the pavement in our Lady Chapell, the pavement in the body of the Churche, the roffe of the cloyster, schingull, and paving stones with the glasse windows, ieron, and paving stones in the Chapter House soulde and only exceptyd

MD.—That the foreseid Mr Willm. Cavendyssh was (put in) possession to our sovereygne lorde the Kyng's use of the scite of the seid late Monastery and all the demaynes to it apperteynyng the xviij day of October, in the xxx yere of our seid sovereygne lorde King Henry viijth.

PENCIONS AND STYPENDS granted to the late Abbott and Convent ther by the seid Commissioners as followyth :—To Robert Watson, late Abbott there, l*li*, and the Mansion of Longdon wyth an acre of grounde adjoyning to the said mansion, and competente tymber for the reparacion of the same house, and also sufficient fyer woode during hys lyfe l*li*. To

> John Hall, vj*li*.
> Richard Cureton, vj*li*.
> Christopher Ledis, cvj*s*. viij*d*.
> T. Maynard, vj*li*.
> Thomas Dawson, cvj*s*. viij*d*
> William Massie, *cs*.
> John Ponsebury vj*li*.
> Peter Robinson *cs*.
> Roger Knowsall, cvj*s* viij*d*.
> Wlm. Stuche cvj*s* viij*d*.
> Sir John Takyll, iiij*li*. vj*s* viij*d*
>
> Totall cix*li*. xiij*s* iiij*d*

FEES AND ANNUITIES granted oute by Convent seale before the tyme of the dissolution of the seid Monastery (including my lord of Shrewsbury, the steward, liij*s*. iiij*d*, to James Michell, for the Kyng's corody, lx*s*.; to William Abbotts, the Kyng's servant, xxvj*s* viij*d*., Thomas Etonn, Esq, xl*s*); summa xix*li* vj*s*. viij*d* Dettes owing by the Abbott and Convent of the seid late Monastery at the dissolution thereof (including to the Archdeacon for procuracions, xxiij*s* iiij*d*; the Church of Lychefelde v*s*.; to the Cathedrall Churche of Coventry, v*s*; to Sir Thomas Dawson for waxe, xviij*s*. iiij*d*; to William Knolles for fyshe of hym bought and not yet payed for x*li*. x*s*. viij*d*., ix chanons for ther habettes dew to them by the late prior ix*li*. x*s*. Summa xxvj*li*. iiij*d*

Annuities and Corrodies.	Nich. Coterell, xls.
	Will. Abbott, xxvls. viii*d*.
	Henry Whitwell, xls.
[A maintenance granted to the nominee of the Crown or some powerful person by a convent	Jas Bordesley, xls.
	John Fisher, lxvis. viii*d*.
	Will. Chorleton, xiiis. iiii*d*.
	Regin Corbett, xxs
Pensions	John Sponeburye, £vi
	Will. Sticke, cvis viii*d*
	Roger Knosall, cvis. viii*d*.
	Thos Maynard, £vi
	Peter Robinson, cs.
	Will Massye, cs.
Fees	Thomas Eyton, steward, xls

ARRANGEMENT OF AUSTIN CANONS' HOUSES.

The contemporaneous description of the Austin Canons' Abbey at Leicester will throw additional light on the arrangement of their buildings, and give us the information in the language of the time.

The Church was on the east side of the Inner Court, fronting a turretted gate house, with chambers on either side, which opened also into an outer Base Court of barns, stables, and houses of husbandry and divers chambers for servants. In the inner court on the S.E. were the bakehouse, brewery, and stables.

Between the west-end of the church and the west-end of the Frater was "a great square house with great chambers and chimneys." The Frater was on the south, and on the east the Dortor, with "stairs leading on high," and "all vaulted under and below, wherein be great large cellars" The Chapter House and Library adjoined it. These buildings inclosed the Cloister square.

Out of the Cloister square an entry conducted to a Hall and chambers, kitchen, and other "houses of office built square about a yard, with galleries above and below" leading to them. A second entry or passage led to the "Fermore" or Infirmary.

At the entrance to the Inner Court from the Base Court there was a tower called the King's Lodgings, having adjacent chambers for the officers in two storeys, with a gallery and a parlour below the great dining chamber at the upper end of a Hall, from which a second gallery communicated with the offices and kitchen These buildings formed the Guest House.

Lyndw
Prov. lib
iii tit 20
S V
observantia
Reyner
P. i 159

The Canons of Lilleshull were of a different branch of the order from those of Haughmond or St. Mary de Pré at Leicester, but the differences in ceremonial were very minute.

Hist. des
Ordres Relig
ii 883

They first settled in England in 1112, and built a house at Grendon Park, being introduced by Walter Giffard, Earl of Buckingham, and Hildegardis, his wife. They ate no meat in Refectory, they wore no shirts, used woollen tunics in their dormitory, and a black habit over a albe or surplice in their ordinary attire. They were founded in 1090, and their earliest home was in the Abbey of the Holy Trinity and S Nicholas, Arouaise, in the diocese of Arras

Wenlock Abbey from N.W.

from a Photograph by J. Jang, Shrewsbury

THE CLUNIAC PRIORY

OF

S. MILBURGA,

Much Wenlock.

---✠---

"A goodly building bravely garnished;
"High lifted up were many lofty towers,
"And goodly galleries far overlaid,
"Full of fair windows and delightful bowers."—Spenser.

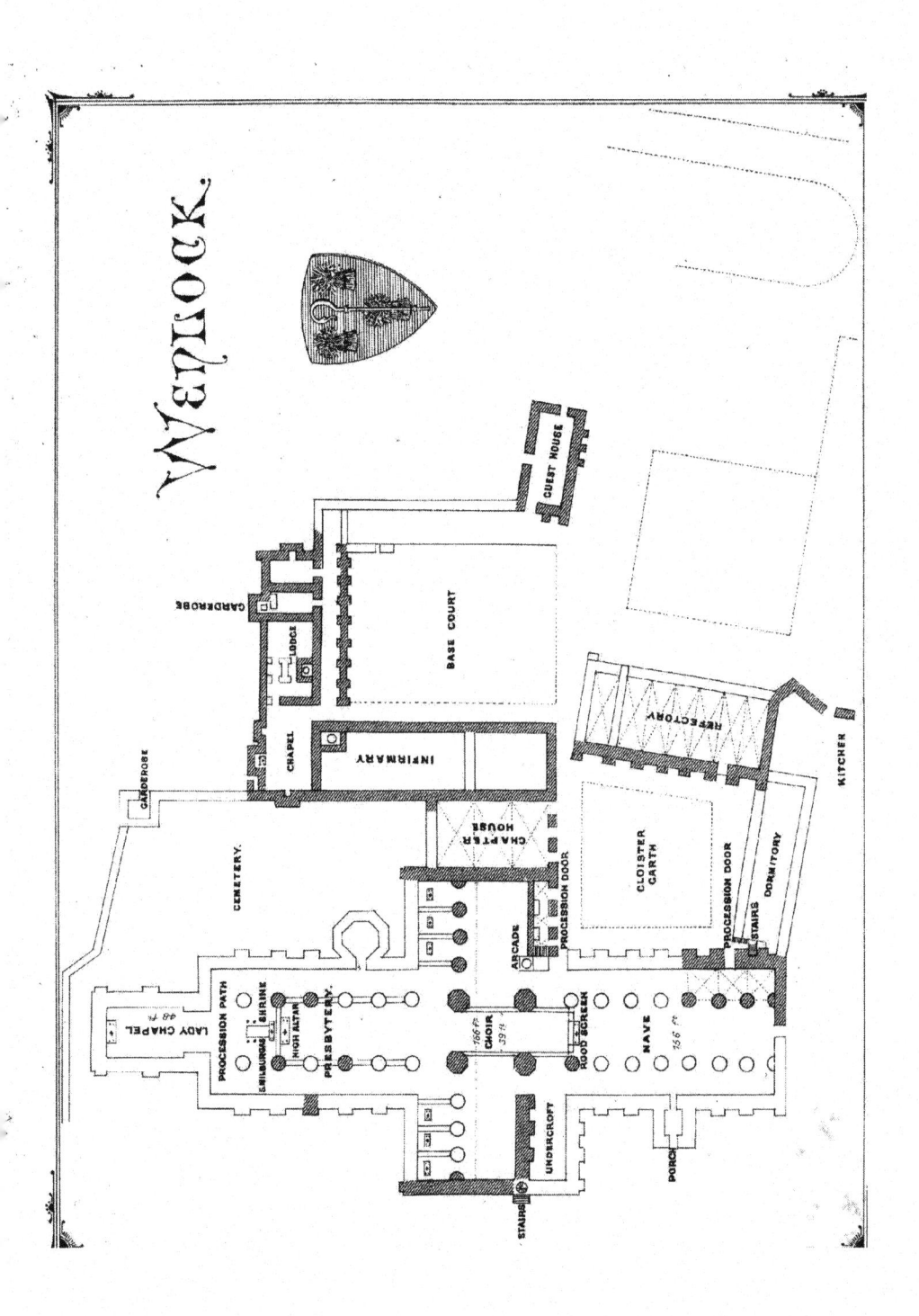

Wenlock.

The Cluniac Priory of S. Milburga, Much Wenlock.

THE railway station of Much or Great Wenlock is approached either by the Herefordshire line under the beautiful heights of Wenlock Edge, or by the winding line from Buildwas and Shrewsbury or Worcester, no less beautiful when the sharp curves reveal the lovely scenery of the steep ascent between wooded hills. From the platform the traveller sees immediately in the valley below him the tall transept gable, with its windows glowing like golden lancets, the tall mass of the southern side of the nave, and the noble galleries and louvre of the abbot's lodge; whilst to the right is seen the grey spire of Holy Trinity, a fine and spacious parish church, Norman and Decorated, rising over the square fragment of the Priory gate house. Beyond it, with a background of rolling hills, pasture and pleasant leas spread out in three broad arms the picturesque roofs and timbered houses of the old town, not the least in interest among the few that in England have as yet escaped the hand of modern innovation. It affords at every turn new subjects for the architectural draughtsman with overhanging storeys, steep gables, carved fronts, deep porches, and quaint chimney-stacks, designed by artistic hands, the chief among all being the Guild Hall, with timber framing which rests on an open pillared corridor beneath

Addit M.S
Brit Mus
27, 765 A,
fo 163

THE MINSTER OF S. MILBURGA.

<small>Giraldus Camb vi 62</small>

Winnicas, Wenlochium (like the Welsh Wenlock or Gwenllwg, in Glamorganshire), and Ventolochium were the first names it bore, until it was long known as Llan Meilien, the town of S Milburga, daughter of Merwald King of Mercia, the fair princess abbess and saint who died here on Feb 28, 722, and the sister of St. Mildred, of Minster in Thanet, whose name is also preserved at Stoke S Milborough William of Malmesbury, thus relates the history of the early church of Wenlock, which was destroyed by the Danes in 874. "There was here a very ancient house of nuns. The place was wholly deserted when Roger, Earl of Montgomery, filled it with Cluniac monks, where now the fair branches of the virtues strain up to heaven The Virgin's tomb was unknown to the new comers, for all the ancient monuments had been destroyed by the violence of the foemen and time. But when the fabric of the new church was commenced, as a boy was running in hot haste over the floor, the grave of the Virgin was broken through and disclosed her body. A fragrant odour of balsam breathed through the church, and her body raised high, wrought so many miracles that floods of people poured in thither Scarcely could the broad fields contain the crowds, whilst rich and poor together, fired by a common faith, hastened on their way None came to return without the cure or mitigation of his malady, and even king's evil, hopeless in the hands of the leech, departed before the merits of the Virgin."

<small>Acta SS iii 388, Reiner P i, pp 62, 63</small>

<small>W Malm de Gestis Reg lib ii c 13</small>

DIFFERENCE BETWEEN CLUNIACS AND CISTERCIANS.

The Cluniacs had no abbeys in England; their homes were simply Priories, dependent upon the foreign mother churches. The Cistercian order was a reform of the Cluniac rule, or rather a revolt from it, so that we have seen that even Giraldus called the early founders of Citeaux Cluniacs instead of Benedictines of Sherborne. The customs, ground plans, and ceremonial were distinct, every Cistercian house was called an abbey in order to protest against the dependent position occupied by the Cluniac priories in this country, and there was almost personal hostility between the members of these widely divergent orders. The dress of the Cluniac was a black woollen frock, a white woollen tunic, and black scapular.

<small>Epist Petri Vener Martene Thesaurus, Vol. v 1569-1654 Antiq Consuet in D'Achery's Spicilegium tom 1 p 641 Liber Cærim Add Ms 29, 606 fo xxxiii</small>

The order differed in ceremonials from the Benedictines. They appeared in England first in 1377, at S Pancras, Lewes They had 34 houses, besides their chief abbeys of Lenton, Montacute, and S. Saviour's, Bermondsey.

<small>Reiner Apost Bened P 1 p 158</small>

THE PRIORY ORIGINALLY ALIEN MADE A DENIZEN.

The earlier church had been "enriched with many ornaments" by Earl Leofric of Mercia, and the Countess Godiva who had proved benefactors to Coventry, Leominster, S. Mary Stow, S Werburgh's and S John's at Chester, Evesham, and Worcester, occupying them probably with secular canons Warren, Earl of Shrewsbury, is also claimed as a founder in 1058. Then Domesday, c. 1080, says "Earl Roger hath made the abbey," he had introduced monks and re-endowed the foundation, which was earlier than the sister house of S Pancras at Lewes, and older than the Benedictine Abbey which he built at Shrewsbury. There was one drawback, the abbey belonged to an order, the smallest and least wealthy in this country, being regarded as un-English and foreign at heart It was (like Bermondsey) a cell or dependency of La Charité sur Loire, (as S. Pancras Lewes was of S. Peter's Clugny), and was charged with a payment to the

<small>Higden Polychronicon 1057 Bromton 949 W Malm. Gesta Pontif s 171 p. 306 Flor Wigorn, s a 1057 Mon Hist Brit p 609 A Ann Wigorn vi 372 Vol 1 p. 252. b</small>

<small>Reyner App P iii s 68 p 147</small>

<small>Ibid P ii p 70 Rymer iii P ii p. 601 (1361)</small>

mother church of a yearly pension ("apportatus)" of 100s. Reyner, the bitter opponent of the order, calls Wenlock "insignis," as Sarum was among Cathedrals. In 1333 it was regarded as the tenth church in England for importance; but four years later, when the goods of Lombards, Cluniacs and Cistercians were confiscated to meet the burden of coming war, Edward III. made the community pay 200s. as an alien cell. In 1361 it was restored to La Carité. On Feb. 20, 1395, by the sacrifice of 600 marks to the Crown, it was, as others had been, naturalized and made a denizen on the condition that the convent celebrated the anniversaries of the King and Queen. Still the foreign step-mother weighed upon it until a Papal bull on Oct. 7, 1494, was issued on the feeble ground that the distance of travelling from Shropshire to La Charité and Clugny was inconvenient, and finally severed its yoke The independence was achieved, but proved all too tardy, for within less than half a century the suppression had taken place.

ARCHITECTUAL FEATURES OF THE MINSTER

A few scanty notices are all that we possess of the architectural history of the minster The eastern arm, always the first portion to be commenced, must have been complete when the body of S. Milburga was translated to a shrine before the high altar on May 26, 1101. The church was still in progress, as Lady Agnes de Clifford in 1222 was a benefactress to the fabric. The Cluniacs in general were "sober and prudent." Such is the testimony of Giraldus Cambrensis, here it is said that they were "most bountiful in alms, and very observant to the rule." They also loved a splendid church, as we learn from the invectives of S. Bernard of Citeaux; the lofty vault, the wide space, the sumptuous glistening smoothness, the curious decking with colour, the rich statuary, the wheel-like circle of lamps, crowns of light sparkling with jewels, and tall candelabra with many branches, offended the severity of the order to which he belonged. The Cluniacs in a spirit of prayer sought to imitate those of the olden time before them, full of knowledge in all manner of workmanship to devise cunning works in gold and silver and brass, in cutting of stones to set them, and in carving of timber.

The contrast must have been very striking which existed between the huge Norman pillars and gloomy greyness of the eastern chapels of Buildwas, and this lighter fabric of Wenlock glowing in sunny brightness, with colour and light, with broad aisles stretching away in the intricacy of the ground plan on every side, rich stained glass mellowed by time, the high vaulting, the foliage on capitals, the deep triforium gallery, the graceful clerestory, the soaring lantern and, receding beyond the gorgeous shrine and ever burning light above the high altar, the distant Lady Chapel faintly seen. The central tower that once seemed to keep guard over the sacred building, contained a peal of bells, three of which still discourse sweet music at Wolverhampton. It is difficult now, standing amid this mutilated wreck, to pourtray even to the liveliest fancy, the scene when they chimed on some high day, and through a great multitude of all conditions the stately procession took its way, novice and monk, two and two, vested in rich copes, and chanting in solemn tones to the sweet sound of the organs and instruments of music, then the prior as beseemed his dignity behind them, cross and banner, taper and cloudy censer going on before.

DESIGN OF CREATING IT A CATHEDRAL CHURCH.

One fact is certain that the building was considered so grand that it was designed to be a cathedral church in union with Shrewsbury by the first

Augm Off Books ? vol. xxiv fo. 74

scheme of Henry VIII. for his new foundations. The chapter was to be composed of 6 prebendaries, with a president, 8 petty canons with gospellar and epistolar; 8 laymen and 8 choristers were to sing and join in the choir Coarse ill-usage has since done its work, and Mayor in the last century has introduced into his view of the abbey a large waggon standing by ready to receive the fragments of a noble column which the spoilers were actually dragging down to patch up some modern house.

DIMENSIONS OF THE MINSTER.

In mere matter of length it more than equals Hereford, and exceeds Rochester amongst our old cathedrals. Glasgow is only longer by 7 feet; but in point of structure and symmetry it must have been a rival to our noblest churches The dimensions were 332 feet; the nave 117ft × 38ft., or with aisles 61ft. 3in., the side walls being 60ft. high The tower occupied a square 48ft. × 46ft The transept was 144ft. from north to south, the aisleless Lady Chapel 41ft × 23ft. On June 6th, 1554 the altar was rebuilt. Ten patterns of tiles have been discovered with the arms of the abbey, *gules*, a raven *or*, a griffin, and others of geometrical or floriated pattern.

THE WEST FRONT.

The southern side of the west front is tolerably perfect, showing the lateral shafts of one of the central windows, forming probably part of a triplet, divided by banded and clustered shafts. Bases of shafts and broken arches only remain to give some faint idea of a grand portal of six orders The front of the aisle is arcaded in three tiers with trefoiled niches and slender

Wenlock Abbey from N.E.

From a Photograph by J. Laing, Shrewsbury.

shafts. A large window of two lights, with a circle in the head, is on the triforium level; below it is a round-headed window.

THE NAVE.

The nave consisted of a tall base arcade, with shafted octagonal pillars, a triforium containing couplets, with nook shafts, and divided by a central group, arranged in front of a wall passage or alure; and an upper or clerestory of similar design but of smaller dimensions The central alley was vaulted, and the clustered shafts rise from small brackets or corbels at the level of the triforium string course. Of all the pillars of the arcade only seven on the south and three on the north remain perfect, in the eastern arm they are circular, and westward of the crossing shafted. For some purpose, probably the provision of a Library, as at Worcester, in a similar position, and at Norwich approximately, the triforium for three bays was enclosed over the south aisle, being parted off on the east and north by solid walls At Wells and in the Grey Friars, London, the library also adjoined the cloister It forms a large chamber with marks of presses and stone benches, and has three two-light windows on the east, west, and south A group of low, stout pillars, with enormous bases and broad Pointed arches, have been added for its support below the original arcade. It communicated by stairs with the Cloister Garth and also with the Dormitory. The door and landing place remain. At the N E. there was access to the triforium. At Benedictine Wymondham the "monks' lodgings were over the south aisle of the nave 76ft × 11ft all leaded." It is possible, however, that here this Chamber may have formed the dormitory of the novices, as their "cella" was separate from the monks according to the rule of the order. The "Minor choir" was the portion of the nave allotted to the novices, and possibly was arranged in the western bays. The portion

Account of Wenlock, by E S A 1853 Arch. Camb, 2 Ser. iv 98 Memoirs in Coll Brit Arch. Assoc and Britton's Arch Antiq v 37·41

L

of the aisle so distinctly marked off from the rest, may have been the place of penitents, as in the foreign churches there was a special western porch for their accommodation, but the only trace of it in this country remains at Lewes

THE SOUTH AISLE.

The SOUTH AISLE has quadripartite vaulting, which in the western bay springs from corbels beautifully tongued, and in the eastern severy from clustered shafts, the capitals are carved with foliage The central compartment is pierced with a Pointed door opening on the Cloister Garth. The rest of the nave-wall on this and on the north side can be readily traced above ground.

THE CROSSING.

Supp of Monast 278 Oliver's Wolverhampton, p 6

The great bases of the crossing must have carried a superb tower of which no tradition survives. Three of its five bells were sold to Wolverhampton in 1540.

THE TRANSEPT —SOUTH WING,

The TRANSEPT retains a large portion of the the SOUTH WING. The front shows a gable pierced with a lancet rising over a triplet, with the central far larger than the lateral lights Three arches, the middle one blind, occupy the triforium, and below them are two fine Pointed arches with a quatrefoil in the central spandril. There is a curious scroll-headed aperture which masks the protrusion of the south wall beyond the arcade of the eastern chapels, and on the west side there is an ingenious arrangement which, at the sacrifice of an aisle conforms the outer wall of the transept to the line of the more ancient Chapter House.

On the west and east sides the triforium consists of couplets, which are contracted in the southernmost bays. The clerestory is composed of single lights, with a continuous label. There is a curious system of square-headed oblong loops to light the wall passages which is very observable.

At the south-west angle there is a curious triplet or canopied arcade; the central part contained a niche for an image, probably of S. Milburga, and a slit for the reception of offerings, as in the stone box at Gloucester, and the standing chest of oak at Chichester. There are two brackets in the lateral niches for images. The spandrils are filled with two small hovels or niches, pointed sharply above, but trigonal in shape below.

The east side has an arcade of three Pointed arches springing from clustered shafts, which once opened into as many CHAPELS, which were divided by parcloses of wood, and had a lean-to roof. The south wall retains a water-drain of peculiar shape; it forms a shouldered arch with a round head.

A somewhat similar instance of arcading remains on what was formerly before the destruction of a chapel the inner wall of the south wing of Pershore Abbey.

THE NORTH WING.

The NORTH WING resembles its fellow. The west wall has three external Pointed arches, with a door at the S.W. angle, near an aumbry. A skew door at the S.E. corner may have led to a staircase, but the principal way to the wall passages was by a vast circular newel, one side of which forms a prominent feature in the angle of the South Wing. On the outside of the west wall a large SACRISTY was erected over a CRYPT. At Thetford there was also a chamber on this side. The Sacristy at Castle Acre was also on the North side, whereas in secular and Benedictine minsters its proper position was on the south

THE PRESBYTERY.

<small>D'Achery Spicilegium 1, 688</small>

The PRESBYTERY retains the bases of three pillars on the south, and two on the north side, and one bay distant from the Transept Chapels there was an octagonal building, 18 feet in diameter, probably the Lavatory, "for the Church use," which is mentioned in the Ancient Uses; an "amphora aquæ de stanno in loco competenti in ecclesia," was supplied for washing the chalices used at low masses At Canterbury there is a circular building approached by

<small>Ib 1, 679</small>

a passage which was supplied with water. A dove for reservation, according to the rule, hung over the high altar. The only other instance on record in an English church was at Salisbury Cathedral. The position of the aumbry

<small>Mon Treas 32, W. Malm Hist Nov 1 4, p 164</small>

behind the altar was another ritual peculiarity of the order The shrine of S. Milburga stood in its usual position, eastward of the high altar. It was taken down by Walter Hendeley, Dr Lee, Richard Bellicis, Richard Watkins, Leonard Beckwith, and William Blithman.

THE LADY CHAPEL.

An aisleless LADY CHAPEL of the middle of the 12th century completed the building.

THE CLOISTER GARTH.—THE TRESAUNT.

On the exterior of the South Wing the three arches are concealed by a shallow detached aisle 4ft. 8in. deep, with three low arches 8ft. 3in. wide towards the cloisters, which are divided by pilaster buttresses. The interspace has quadripartite vaulting. It was an ingenious architectural device to mask a defect of plan, as a whole aisle was absorbed into the east cloister alleys of Oxford and Westminster, but it was made available probably as a parlour, an aumbry for cloister books, and seats for the Maundy like the recessed stone benches of Worcester. Its technical name was the Tresaunt, a term elsewhere applied to a cloister alley, or a passage from it.

When the monks left the Chapter House they formed two lines, and sat down in the cloister to be shaved on certain days, one half of the convent being placed against the wall, facing their brethren "ad cancellos clustri" in the seats within the windows, and leaving the space vacant before the Chapter House and Church door.

<small>Liber Cærim. Add. MS. Brit. Mus. 20, 666, fo. xxxiii.</small>

THE CHAPTER HOUSE.

The richest building which now exists is the roofless CHAPTER HOUSE, Transitional Norman, an oblong 51ft. × 25ft. 6in. The Western entrance consists of three large round arches, which have lost their shafts, with these ornaments, the wave, the chevron, and indented in the mouldings. The abaci have hearts, scales, chevrons and garlands, and the capitals are relieved by a fretty and other patterns. In the north spandril is a figure, later by a century, of S. Peter with his keys, which formerly was counterpoised by S. Paul. Above the portal four large round-headed windows once gave light to this room. The eastern wall is nearly gone. The remaining portions are 21ft. above the ground. It is of three bays divided by groups of six shafts, massive and low, and sub-divided into five spaces by intersecting arches in three tiers with diagonal masonry in the spandrils above. The lowest tier rising above a chevroned string course, is beaded and encloses an arcade like stall-work (which it was, not) of five chevroned arches in each bay, and four-leaved flowers within diamonds on the jambs. The capitals display every variety of fanciful design and a profusion of capricious play of the imagination on the south, but on the north the sculptures have never been completed, and the decoration is scanty; except on the groups of pillars from which the broad ribs of the vaulting rose These have elaborate carvings on their capitals, forming a continuous pattern, whereas the rest, except in the eastern bay, are simply scolloped. On the south side, near an aperture or recess of the same shape, there is a square-headed recess or door with a mask between two gigantic lizards.

SOUTH SIDE OF THE CLOISTER GARTH.
THE REFECTORY.

The gabled west wall of the Infirmary completes this side of the Cloister Garth On the south are remains of the REFECTORY, 85 × 32, once vaulted in seven spans. These consist of the doorway from the cloister, a few fragments of vaulting shafts, and two round-headed aumbries. With the usual carelessness of Cluniac ground plans, especially at Bromholm and Lewes, the Refectory does not lie parallel with the Church, nor does the DORMITORY with the Chapter House The novices came and fetched their fare to their cell from the Regular Kitchen, whilst the unconsecrated hosts after mass were distributed in the Refectory

Add MS
Brit Mus
29, 540

D'Achery
Spicil. 1.
p 44,702 679

WEST SIDE OF CLOISTER GARTH.

The Dormitory, standing over a substructure, adjoined the south-west angle of the church, and on the west side of the Refectory projecting beyond the line of this undercroft, the round arched doorway of the kitchen remains. The Cluniacs introduced the decent practice of dividing the Dormitory into separate cells by wooden partitions.

COURT OF THE INFIRMARY AND GUEST HOUSE.

At the S.E. angle of the Refectory there is a two storeyed building retaining a large pointed arch which encloses two low shouldered arches, some doors and square-headed windows. The Infirmary at Castle Acre was also on the S E. of the cloister. This room was probably part of the Guest House, and formed the west side of the Court of the INFIRMARY, which still remains on the north with its Norman door and range of six round-headed lancets. A short wing crossing above the two western bays of the Chapter House, as the position of a shaft in its east end shows, communicated by square doorways with the triforium of the south wing.

THE PRIOR'S LODGE.

On the east side of this Court is the PRIOR'S LODGE, a two storeyed building with a tall roof and a picturesque prospect-turret. It affords the most interesting example of the domestic arrangements of the house of the superior of a great religious community which we possess It is of the latter part of the 15th century, and consists of a large western gallery 100ft long, in two storeys, over which the roof is carried down as a cover. It has open windows in trefoiled couplets, with mullions and transoms, and is buttressed; the corridors being connected by a wide newel staircase. At each end there is a chimney. On the ground floor, reckoning from north to south, there is an oratory (with an altar having seven niches, and a water drain recessed within an oriel,) lighted by a triplet window. The chamber above may have opened laterally upon it,

<small>Turner's Domes. Arch II, 145, 306 368</small>

to form a gallery, whilst a lofty screen, probably veiled the little sanctuary. Upon the altar is laid a lectern with rude Norman foliage, somewhat resembling one found at Evesham. Beyond the oratory southward are an Entry, Kitchen and Brewhouse. Over these is the Prior's Refectory for the entertainment of guests, with a carved ceiling, and brackets at the sides of the windows, which once had figures of saints painted on the wall above the dais. To it succeeds the Parlour with its waterdrain and garderobe formerly screened off by a timber closure. The projecting water drains from the upper floor were wrought into the semblance of lions' heads and grotesque forms The dormitories or sleeping apartments were over head. The eastern front has long narrow windows, divided by a single mullion double transomed, and with acutely pointed triangular heads

THE ALMONRY GATE.

<small>Blakeway's MS
Duke's MS
fo 543
Val Eccles
III, 216
Min. Acc. 100
Wenlock 32,
33, Henry
VIII. m 1</small>

The ALMONRY was just opposite the GATEHOUSE into the precinct, on one side of which was the porter's lodge and the prison of the franchise. A house was built over it in 1577. It was double-gabled, and now retains a door with a shouldered arch and some small windows in a square solid tower On every Friday here bread at a cost of 40 shillings, on every Sunday 11*d*. in the King's name; every Sunday 10*s*. in bread and beer, on Maunday Thursday bread and fish, 14*s* worth of bread on Wednesday in Holy Week, and loaves costing 30s. on Tuesdays in Lent were distributed to the poor

THE ENDOWMENTS OF THE PRIORY.

<small>Extenta
Tempor. 43.
Edw III
Add. MS
6165. fo. 97</small>

And this is all that can be told of this great Priory, which had pastures on the Clees, woods at Spexhull, Ditton, and Shirlot, hayes for game, vivaries

COPIED FROM BUCK'S VIEWS, 1731.

W

NLOCK.

for fish, and a park at Oxenbold and Madeley. Eighteen thousand goodly acres made up its manors at Godstock, Doddington, Dehocsele (Degxhill), Nehelworde, Easton-under-Heywood, Erdington, Pelelic, Pickthorn, Sutton, Cakeley, Wolverton, Middeley, King's Stanton, Bockington, Newton, Calweton, Bouleton, Downton, the More, and with names telling of their occupiers, Monks' Hall, Monks' Hopton, Monks' Mughall, and Monks' Weston.

Pat. Rot 18 Edw. I, m 21. Inq. ad quod damn. 9 Edw II

Various services were due to the Prior by the custom of the manor. At the assizes in the 13th century the men of Wenlock were, save seven, declared to be de dominio prioratus, and it is added non possunt placitare per breve de libero tenemento.

Esch. 31 Hen III n 42. 56 Hen III rot 9

It possessed the right of a fair on S. John Baptist's day, the eve and morrow, at Wenlock, and another at Madeley, a market on Monday at Wenlock, and a second at Eton, which brought in a good revenue from the rent of booths and tolls. Bishop William de Vere gave to it the churches of Wenlock and S Edith's Eatun, in consideration of the Monks' hospitality, requiring them only to provide chaplains Prene Priory was a dependent cell; S. Helen's, in the Isle of Wight, before 1155, was subjected to it, being two of those small houses in which the inmates were withdrawn from the strict rule, and discipline was subject to irreparable decay. St. James', Dudley, was affiliated by Gervase Paganel in 1180, and it colonised Paisley with Prior Humbald and 13 monks in 1164, with 13 monks at the desire of Walter Fitz Alan. It held many churches, St. John Baptist's, Dilton Priors, S. Swithin's, Clunbury; S. Mary, Waterdine; S. Mary, Clinton; S. Mary, Oppetune, Eggedune, and Sibsune, St. James', Shipton; S. George's and S. Thomas, Clun, with seven chapels, the gift of Isabella de Saye, wife of William

Fines 11 Hen III, m 9 Cart. 3, Edw. III, n 222.

Fines 29, Hen III Escaet 29 Hen III. m 103,

Walcott's Scoti Monasticon, p. 295 Pat. Rot 22 Edw III m 12 18 Rich II, p 2, m 29.

Botterel, in the reign of K. Stephen; St. Peter's, Monk's Hopton; St Giles', Barrow; Acton Road, S. Mary's Doddington, S. Michael's Madeley; Stoke St. Milborough; and St. Milburga, Beckbury.

Ann. Wigorn, iv 487
Blakeway's MS ii
Rot. Pat. 37 Henry VIII p. iii, 13 Eliz p. iv m 192

In the twelfth century it had 40 monks; in 1374 they had fallen to 17. Want of discipline seems to have occurred, although it was confederated with Worcester for mutual help and prayers in 1253. The honest Benedictine chronicler relates under the date of August, 1283, that one William, late a brother of Wenlac, but afterwards captain of banditti, being taken with a horse, was led to judgment, at Oswaldeslawe, by troopers and armed men, for fear of a rescue by other robbers, and there he met his due reward.

Part of Grant Pub Rec Office

In 1291 the monastic income was £144, in 1346 it was £237 4s 2½d At the surrender it was valued at £449 net, or, according to some calculations, £401 0s 7¼d, when it was granted to Cardinal Wolsey's physician, Augustine de Augustine, doctor of physic, Prebendary of York, Aug. 5, 1530. After the surrender on Jan 26, 1540, the Prior retired on £80 a year The physician sold the site to Thomas Lawley; his descendant, Robert Bertie, sold it to Lord Gage; Viscount Gage alienated it to Sir William Wynn, and by an interchange of property it now belongs to Mr. Gaskell.

Cole MS xxvi 249
Salop Records vi 247

PRIORS OF WENLOCK

Peter.
Rainald, sat in the Council of Rheims 1148. W. of Wycombe, dedicated his life of Bp. Betun to him.
1166.—Humbert, or Wynebald.
Peter de Leiâ consecrated Bishop of S. David's Nov. 7, 1176.
Henry.
John.

Robert 1192-7
Joybert, Prior of Daventry and Bermondsey, retired as Prior of Coventry Jan., 1198.
1221—Richard.
Humbert, or Imbert, 1221-60, frequently employed as an envoy on Foreign Missions.
May 8, 1260—Aymo de Montibus, prior of Bermondsey; had the custody of Northampton Priory; died 1272.
1265—Guyscard
1272—John de Tyeford, or Thefford, prior of S. Andrew's, Northampton.
Feb. 26, 1320.—Guichard de Cherlieu, prior of Northampton.
1325—Henry de Bonville, or Northam, prior of Bermondsey.
Humbert c, 1348.
Henry de Myons, or de Chay, 1360.
Otto de Fleury, c. 1371
William de Pontefract, c. 1376.
Roger Wyvill, c 1395
Jan. 18, 1397.—John Stafford
Roger Norris died 1421.
1421—William de Peyton *a*
July 11, 1435.—William Brugge (Bridgenorth) resigned.
May 12, 1438—Roger Barry. *b*
1462.—William Walwyn
July 11, 1462.—Roger Wenlock
Oct. 16, 1468.—John Stratton. *c*
July 9, 1471.—John Shrewsbury.
John Wenlock died 1479.
1479—John Shrewsbury again resigned 1481. *d*
April 21, 1482—Thomas Tutbury.
1485.—Richard Syngar.
1511.—Richard Wenlock *e*
July, 1521—~~Richard Gracewell~~

a. Harl MS 2179 fo. 14. 250.

b. Orig 16 Hen VI rot 32.

c Orig 8, Edw VI., rot 29

d 11 Edw VI, rot 49 Ed v IV, rot 16

e Harl MS 2155, fo 67 Add MS 21151 fo 167

<small>Inv of Moche Wenlock.
6 Ed VI,
Ch Goods
Salop 8/13</small>

Dec, 1526—John Bayley, or Cressage, died at Madeley Manor House, on Christmas Day, 1553, buried there on the morrow, but not in accordance with his own wish, for I find the following entry:—"A cope of red and blewe tafata inbrodered with gold and sylver, gave to the paroche by Sir John Bailey, late prior there, in condicion that part of the paroche should at his decesse mete his bodis att Byldwas brigge and bryng hym to Wenloke Churche to be buried"

The surrender was made Jan 26, 1539, and the monks were pensioned

<small>Aug Off Misc Book,
vol 234, fo. 253</small>

John Baylie, sub-prior, £80.
William Corfelde, £6 13s 4d
Richard Fishwyke, £6 13s. 4d.
Thomas Acton, £6 13s. 4d
John Castell, £6 0s. 0d
Richard Fenymer, £6 0s. 0d
William Benge, £6 0s 0d
Richard Norgrove, £6 0s. 0d.
William Morthowe, £5 6s 8d.
John Lee, £5 6s 8d
William Chamberlyn, £5 6s 8d
Thomas Ball, £5 6s. 8d
John Hopkyns, £5 6s 8d.

<small>Exch QR,
Misc. Book,
vol. 32, fol xlix</small>

Wenlock Annuities and Corrodies.

Rich and Kath. Neele, xxvs.
Thos Love, lxvis. viiid
Will. Charleton, xiiis. iiiid.
Will Scudemore, xls.
Jo Smalman, xiiis. iiiid
Rob Warrington, xls.
Ralph Lee, liiis iiiid
Rich., Fras. and Thos. Lawley, vili.
Rich. Wrotesley, liiis iiiid.
Ralph Patenson, xxvis. viiid.

Will. Langley al. Lawley. lxs,
Rich Oseley, xiiis iiiid.
Clements Throgmorton, assignatione Johannis Reynoldes, xls
Hugh Morall, lxxviiis. xd
Fras Broke, xiiis iiiid.
Will Shesdall, cs.
Andrew Walton, xls
Thomas Harnage, xxs.
John Lawley, xls
John Felde, xls.
Rowland Gesnell, nuper Prioris per nomen annuitatis super resignatione ibidem, lxxxli.
Rob. Little and Will. Mounslowe, cs.
Jo. Laking, lxs

Penc Rich. Fenymer vili
Will Benge, vili
Will. Morthowe, cvis. viiid.
Jo Leighe, cvis. viiid.
Thos Balle, cvis. viiid
John Hopkins. cvis. viiid.

Fees. Fras. Earl of Shrewsbury, chief steward, 3li.
Edward Lodge, clk receiver gen , xiiis. iiiid.
„   „   auditor, xls

The following list of the inmates of monasteries at their dissolution taken from unpublished records in the Public Record Office, will illustrate the relative importance of the Salopian houses.—

Benedictine.—Canterbury Cathedral, 69 ; S Augustine's, Canterbury, 32; Bury S. Edmund's, 44; Tewkesbury, 48; Worcester Cathedral, 41 ; S. Benet., Hulme, 24, Glastonbury, 42; Colchester, 17 ; Winchcombe, 25,

Croyland, 36, Pershore, 22; Abingdon, 26; Bardney, 14; Chertsey, 15; Wymondham, 11, Tynemouth, 19, Tavistock 21; S. Alban's, 39, Milton, 13; Brecon, 6, Bardney, 12, Abbotsbury, 10, Hyde 21; Cerne, 17; Sherborne, 17, Norwich Cathedral, 18, Coventry Cathedral, 18; Battle, 19.

Cistercian —Roche, 18, Merevale, 10; Billesden, 11, Furness, 30; Croxden. 13; Bordesley, 19; Ford, 14, Holm Cultram, 25; Rievaulx, 23, 23, Vale Royal, 15, Warden, 14; Byland, 25, Bindon, 8; Beaulieu, 21; Buildwas, 12

Austin Canons.—Haughmond, 11, Lilleshull, 11, Thornton, 25, Walsingham, 22; Cirencester, 21; Bisham, 16, Bradenstoke, 14, Bruton, 15, Kirkham, 18, Tarent, 19, S German's, 8; Ulvescroft, 8, Newstead, 12, Newburgh, 18, Leicester, 20, Llanthony, 25, Kenilworth, 18, S. Osyth's, 16, Dale 17, Bolton, 15, Worksop, 14; Waltham, 19; Bristol, 19.

Cluniac.—Wenlock, 14); Thetford, 14

Præmonstratensian —Sulby, 12; Torre, 16.

The ineffectual scheme of a Salopian see, defeated by the King's avarice, was as follows —

Shrewsbury cum Wenlock

<small>Misc Book, Court of Augm xxiv, fo 26</small>

A bishope, a president, xl*li*., vi prebendaries, every of them, xx*li*. by the yere, a reader of Divinity, xx*li*., viii petite canons to singe in the queyre, every of them viii*li* by the yere; viii laymen to singe and serve in the quyre, every of them vi*li*. xiii*s* iiii*d*.; viii choristers, every of them by the yere iii*li*. vi*s*. viii*d*,; a gospeller vi*li*, a pistoler, v*li*., twoo sextons vi*li*. xiii*s*. iiii*d*., a master of the children x*li*. There was to be a reader of Divinity at 60*li*, and a domus fund for repairs, of 30*li*; a barber porter, a butler, a chief and under cook, a cater, 8 almsmen, etc. Lewis Thomas was consecrated at Lambeth, as suffragan of S. Asaph, bishop of Shrewsbury, on June 28th, 1537, by the Primate and Bishops of Rochester and S. Asaph. He was Cistercian Abbot of Cymmer, B.C.L. of Oxford, 1534, and rector of Llan Twroc, Sept. 26th, 1537. He died in 1560.

Ath. Oxon. II 277 Fasti 95. Strype's Cranmer 87, 1046. Percival Apost. Succ. App.

The arms of the Priory were (1) within a bordure *gu.* and *arg.*, an inescutcheon, *or* (2), *arg.* three garbs, *2 and 1*; in pale a pastoral staff, *or*.

The seals of the Priory of the 14th century are in the British Museum (83 D.3) and the Public Record Office, (B. 469) and drawn in Gent. Mag. 76. P.I. 107.

The name of an abbey was popularly given to several priories, not only in England, but on the continent, and to this time the custom lingers at Wenlock, Carlisle, and Bath.

CONCLUSION.

I could from my own reading among the letters in the State Papers give a painful story of the dissolution and the conduct of Cromwell, his visitors and creatures, but I prefer to use the words of authors of established reputation for honesty and accuracy, who lived nearer to those times, and had no predilections for monk or canon regular. Bishop Godwin, commenting on the righteous fall of Cromwell, says that wise and godly men could not approve the destruction of so many grand churches, built for the worship of God by our ancestors, even to the ground, the diversion of such an amount of ecclesiastical revenues to private use; and the abolition of every place where men might lead a religious life in peace and retirement from worldly business devoting themselves wholly to literary toil and meditation.

<small>Annales Anglici lib 1 Ad Ann 1540.</small>

<small>Kennet II, 1886</small>

Lord Herbert himself is compelled to admit that "some societies behaved themselves so well as their life being not only exempt from notorious faults, but their spare time bestowed in writing books, painting, carving, graving, and the like exercises, that their visitors became intercessors for them," though Cromwell with much violence said "their houses should be thrown down to the foundations."

<small>Britannia I cxxxiv</small>

"Till the reign of Henry VIII.," Camden writes, "there were monuments of the piety of our ancestors erected to the honour of God, the propagation of Christianity and learning and support of the poor, religious houses to the number of 645. About the 36th year of King Henry VIII a storm burst upon the English Church like a flood, breaking down its banks which, to the astonishment of the world and grief of the nation, bore down the greatest part of the religious with their fairest buildings These were almost all shortly after destroyed, their revenues squandered away, and the wealth which the Christian piety of the English had from the first conversion of England dedicated to God in a moment dispersed, and, if I may be allowed the expression, profaned."

Strype, no lover of the regular, but their bitter-tongued enemy, is fain to confess that "the common people well liked the greater monasteries, and generally were very fond of them, because of the hospitality and good housekeeping there used. The inhabitants of these cloisters relieved the poor, raised no rents, took no excessive fines upon renewing of leases, and their noble and brave built structures adorned the places and countries where they stood The rich also had education here for their children."

Memorials I, 1533

Stowe honestly says that the visitors in October, 1535, "put forth all religious persons that would goe, and all that were under the age of foure and twenty yeeres, and after closed up the residue that would remaine, so that they should not come out of their places. All religious men that departed the abbot or prior to give them for their habit a priest's gown and 40s of money They tooke out monasteries and abbes their chiefest jewels to the King's use." At the dissolution of the Lesser Houses (which were legally and very often advisedly dissolved) in the following year "the moveable goods were sold Robin Hoode's pennyworths, and the religious persons that were in the said houses were clearly put out, some went to other greater houses, some went abroad to the world It was a pitiful thing to hear the lamentation that the people in the countrey made for them, for there was great hospitality kept among them, and as it was thought more than 10,000 persons, masters and servants, had lost their livings by the putting down of those houses at that time" The

Chron 572

spoilers of Winchester, touched with a passing shame, informed their employer that they began to have misgivings that the people would think that they "came more for treasure than for the abomination of idolatry." The godless King and his minions shared the spoil; but the poor have suffered to this hour, the spirit of devotion for holy things and places received a shock from which even now it only slowly recovers, and the land is covered with scars.

> Denique non lapides quoque vinci cernis ab ævo,
> Non altas turres ruere et putrescere saxa,
> Non delubra Deûm simulacraque fessa fatisci,
> Nec sanctum numen fati protollere fines
> Posse, neque adversus naturæ fœdera niti ?
> Denique non monumenta virum dilapsa videmus,
> Æraque propoero solidumque senescere ferrum ?
> —*Lucretius V. 306-312*

In parting with the subject we see that there were grave and weighty, national and religious causes in the face of "superstitious ignorance," foreign usurpation, and unauthorised accretions on doctrines, practice, and historic faith, which demanded general and immediate reform of evils and abuses Wykeham, years before, had mourned over the decay of discipline; Chichele, Henry VI, and Wolsey had suppressed some of the lesser houses, an internecine feud divided the orders, and set regular against secular, whilst popular disfavour and suspicion had grown in force between the time of Chaucer and the Homilist, so that it required only the scandalous misrepresentation of compliant visitors, creatures of a godless man, to include all in one indiscriminate condemnation The lesser houses were legally dissolved by Act of Parliament The exemption from diocesan authority, the broad lands and ample revenues of the Benedictines, and the unkingly falsehood that the army should be maintained and the taxes defrayed out of the confiscated income prevailed to their destruction. But abbots and priors, monks and canons died for their faith The noble, the courtier, and the powerful were bribed, and falsehoods were spread abroad. Then the tyrant King forced against law, conscience and right the greater houses to make surrender to the Crown. Several heads of religious houses became diocesan and suffragan bishops.

A royal scheme for the conversion of many a fair abbey into a new see for the pure worship of God, Evangelical preaching and Christian education which exists on paper in the Public Record Office took partial effect in the case of Chester, Peterborough, Gloucester, Bristol, Oxford, and Westminster.

In the Cathedrals of the New Foundation many a monk, refuting by his presence the base slanders of the time, retained his old stall, but in vain Bishop Lee, with the whole city joining in his suit, had pleaded for his noble see at Coventry, in vain Knightly and the other faithful three prayed the King to stay his hand if he "had any remorse that any religious house should stand as meet for its gracious charity and pity." The other houses of God might become quarries, factories or lay stalls, when not clean swept off the earth "Saints and angels in leathern pouch" were all that the wicked wanton spoiler cared for In vain Lord Chancellor Audley pleaded for Colchester and S Osyth's In vain Latimer besought that some of these houses, filled with inmates not bound by vows and revived under stringent statutes might be "left for preaching, study and prayer in every shire." State Papers, 1587 Cotton MS Cleop. F v, 264

It is no wonder that we find the ancient minsters so utterly wrecked, for Henry VIII. fortified Calshot Castle with the stones of Beaulieu and Netley, and in 1549 Edward VI. ordered "20 ffoder of lead to be had out of the late monastery of Glastonbury to be employed about the King's Castle of Jersey." One thousand fodder were sent beyond the seas, and all that was dispersed throughout the realm was to be collected for the king. Five hundred Council Register 11 143 145 loads of stone were taken out of the steeple of S. Edmund's Bury to repair the town walls and West Bridge.

> I do love these ancient ruins,
> We never tread upon them but we get
> Our foot upon some reverend history.
> And questionless here in this open court,
> Which now lies naked to the injuries
> Of stormy weather, some men lie interred,
> Loved the Church so well, and gave so largely to it,
> They thought it should have canopied their bones
> Till Domesday. But all things have their end ;
> Churches and cities which have diseases like to men,
> Must have like death that we have.—*Webster.*

ADDITIONAL NOTES.

BUILDWAS.

P 11 —The charter of confirmation by K Stephen is dated, "apud Salopesburiam in obsidione." The charter of confirmation I Ric takes note of the collecta bladi quæ vocatur Church omber in the hundreds of Wrocwurthin and Cundure"

P. 19 —"The answer of an abbot of this house to K. Hen. iii. is remarkable Matthew Paris has it A D. 1256"

P 11 —Osbert, the son of William, lord of Strichele, gave his capital messuage of Stirchley with sixty acres of land, " ita quod nihil mechi vel heredibus meis de tota villa de Stircheley retinuerim præter orationem et suffragia domus de Buldewas." 6 Pat 13 Edw I. m 28. Cart. 20 Edw. I n 39, 40, 41, Pat 18 Hen. vi p 3, m. 10 The monastery obtained the King's confirmation. Escheat 14 Edw I n 58 The abbot gave the manors of Kennerton, Ruton, and Sherheste to Richard, Earl of Arundel, in exchange for Cunede Church. Pat. 28, Edw III. p 22, m 22

P. 21.—This Visitors' door is found also at Tintern and Abbey Dore, and in a corresponding position at Valle Crucis and Furness.

P. 26 —The King granted the site and precinct to Lord Powis Orig 8. p 37, Hen. VIII. rot 114.

Salop Record vol 1
Add MS
Brit Mus
21,019, ff 151-4,

HAUGHMOND

P 32.—When the Abbot of Haughmond made his visitation of Ranton Priory, in Staffordshire, he was to be entertained for one night.

P. 39.—Pat. Rot. 28 Hen. III. m 3. John L'Estrange and the Prior of Wenlock were empowered to renew the truce with David, son of Llewellyn, late Prince of North Wales.

C Bundel Brev. 1. Edw. 1.—The abbots of Dore and Haughmond were authorised to receive the fealty due from the Prince of Wales to the King, but that Prince not appearing at the time and place, the abbots certified the same to the Lord Chancellor.

At the Assizes 20 Edward 1, the grant of Chesworthyn Church by Henry III was produced by the abbot, and the vill of Walecote was proved to have been given by the Empress Maud in frank almaigne.

The advowson of Wroxeter was confirmed 14 Edw III.

Abbot Alured procured from P. Alexander III a bull allowing mass to be said in a low voice, without ringing of bells in time of interdict.

Staines is now called Stone, in Staffordshire.

Abbot Nicholas, in 1332, built a new kitchen for the use of the Convent, with a cook to dress their food, and allotted the churches of Hunstanton and Ruyton, the parks, the Priors and Saleispark to supply it with meat, fish and lard

"Abbott Ralph granted a corrody to one of his squires to maintain a servant and two horses, which was the common equipage that squires of this abbey appeared with"

Pope Boniface IX. (1389-1404) granted special indulgences for penitents who visited the Church on certain feasts

Hen. V. (1420-1)—"Richard Burnel, canon, was elected abbott. He gave the prior precedency next to the abbott, and in his absence permission to be served with covered dishes at table, which was the usual state of the abbott's service."

Henry de Astley received the temporalities Dec 4, Rot Pat 9 Edw. I, p 1

Gilbert de Campeden received the king's assent July 27, Rot Pat 12, Edward 1, resigned Rot. Pat. 33 Edw. I, p 1.

Engelard resigned 30th April. G. Prior of Stanes, succeeded Aug. 4 Rot Pat. 25 Hen III, m. 4

Licencia eligendi abbatem de Haghmon per mortem Rogeri Westeley Jan 15. Rot. Pat. 9, Hen V. p 2.

Salop Rec 1
Add Ms
Brit Mus,
21, 019, ff 121
123

P. 41.—The revenue and endowments were confirmed by Pat. Rot. 13 Edw 1 p. 22, m. 12 "Some of the princes of Wales had been benefactors of monastery, upon which account this abbott was in greater esteem among the Welch than any other regular in these parts.

Richard, Earl of Arundel, in 1392, bequeathed to Chichester Cathedral one hundred marks et a l' abbey de Hamound per mesme la manere cent marcs, issint q'il soit veu per mes ditz executours qe les ditz somes soient exploitez (expended) en ascune chose come soit en l' onour de Dieux et amendement des ditz meisouns, sy ceo ne poet estre perpetuel, qar (car) je averoie meulx qe ceo serriot parpetuelment adurer, qe autrement sy ceo purra bien estre coment qe ceo serroit bien poy (very near) de tielx sommes.

Nichol's Royal
and Noble
Wills, p. 127.

LILLESHULL.

P. 53.—" Other authorities tell us that there was here a religious house of Secular Canons in the time of the Saxon dynasty, and afterwards became a nunnery, which was reduced to a state of desolation by the predatory incursions of the Welsh tribes, and so continued till about the year 1145."

P. 54.—There can be no doubt that the mediæval builders loved to bring in nature as it were a worshipper into the sanctuary and hallow the course of the seasons and the operations of man's hands by introducing them on misericord; round capitals as at Carlisle; on portals as at Malmesbury; or upon the ceilings as at Salisbury. The following lines, prefixed to the several months in the Church Kalendar of the MS. Breviary of S. Alban's Abbey, suggest a clue to the right reading of these often curious or quaint sculptures, carvings or portraitures which have been misread or unexplained :—

> Pocula Janus amat, Februarius algeo clamat;
> Martius arva fodit; Aprilis florida nutrit;
> Ros et flos nemorum Maio sunt fomes amoris;
> Junius dat fena; Julio resecatur avena;
> Augustus spicas, September colligit uvas;
> Seminat October; spoliat virgulta November;
> Queris habere cibum porcum mactando December.

Another reading is—

> October vina prebet cum carne ferina.

P. 56.—The Austin Canons' Church of Dunstable has also a Perpendicular superstructure to a north-west tower.

P. 59.—Hillaria de Trusse, but first the wife of Robert de Budlers, gave several parcels of land "ad coquinariæ sustentationem et ad augmentum victus in refectoris."

P. 62.—A charter Cart. I. John p. i. m. 121 recites the possessions of the house, but the largest account of the revenues is expressed in the confirmation, Pat. 18 Ric. II. p. 1, m. 7. There are also particulars of account of the temporalities by John Wenlok, abbot, after the resignation of the abbot, William Lege. Wenlok was still abbot 18 Edw IV

The Church of Badminton was given 14 Edw III. p 2 m 31.

Salop Records
1 Add MS
Brit Mus,
21,019. if
253 6

The Hospital of S John at Bridgnorth was put under the abbot. Pat. Rot. 1 Edw. IV p 2 m 16 "The house lying near the Chester Road, the abbots were sometimes known to complain that their income was too scanty for the entertainment of the passengers that travelled that road."

Allan resigned The King gave his consent to the election of **W de Dorleg,** April 12. Rot Pat 10 Hen III

Simon died in December Rot Pat 25 Hen. III.

Robert de Arkalaw had the King's assent June 15. 37 Hen. III., m. 8

William de Hales, prior, received the temporalities Dec 16. Rot Pat. 55 Hen. III

William de Hales resigned Luke de Salop received the temporalities Sept 4 Rot Pat 3 Edw. I, m. 10

P 63 —Ralph de Salop received the temporalities June 22 Rot Pat. 12, Edward I.

Ralph de Salop resigned William de Bruge received the temporalities May 9 Rot Pat 20, Edw I

William de Poppelowe, rex assentit electioni Mau 17. temporalia restitua 3 June Rot Pat 27, 27 Edw I p 1

John de Chetenwynde resigned Henry de Stoke received the temporalities Aug. 2. Rot. Pat. 4, Edw, III p. i.

William Penytone received the temporalities March 7. Rot. Pat 49. Edward III., p. 1 On his death William Lye had the temporalities Feb. 12. Rot Pat 21, Rich II, p 3

John Wenlock had the king's assent July 27. Rot Pat 10 Hen. VI. p. 2

Robert Fitzjohn had the temporalities restored 19 July. Rot. Pat. 4 Edw IV, p 1 He was living 19 Edw IV.

TABLE OF CONTENTS.

BUILDWAS ABBEY.

ITS Dedication—Derivation of the Name—Of the Order of Savigny it becomes Cistercian, 1, p. 9 Account of the Order—Its Character, p 10 Endowments of the Abbey—The Cope of Fair Rosamond—Burning of the Minster by the Welsh, 11. Grant of a Quarry and Felling Wood in Shirlot Forest—Town House at Lichfield—The Abbot and the King a Question of Alms—Dependent Abbeys. Basingworth—St Mary's, Dublin, Dunbrody, 12 S Mary, Port St Mary—Right of Visitation of Strat Marcell—List of the Abbots—Resignation of the Abbey, 13 Annuities and Corrodies—MS of the Abbey in Shrewsbury School Library—Grant of the Site, p 14 Ground Plan of the Abbey—The Nave—Symbolism of the Arcade—Austere Character of Architecture, p 15 Arrangement of the Choir Stalls—p 16—and The Western Inner Porch—The Rood Screen Division into Choirs of the Monks- the Infirm and Converts—The Lantern Tower, p 17 The Transept and Eastern Chapels—Staircase to the Tower Dormitory Night Stairs—Doorway to the Sacristy—The Presbytery, p 18 The Sedilia, Undercroft of the Transept, p 19 The Watch by the Bier of the Dead—The Cloister Garth—Peculiar Position of the Cloisters, p 20 Arrangement of the West Side and of the East Side—The Sacristy, p 21 The Chapter House—Symbolism of the Five Windows—Use of the Chapter House—The Cloisters had a Pent Roof, p 22 Slype to the Cemetery—The Dormitory—The Common Hall p 24 The Calefactory—Subordinate Buildings—The Infirmary, p. 25 Arrangement of the Hall and Chapel, The Abbot's Lodge, p 26 Use of the Calefactory, p 27

HAUGHMOND ABBEY.

Derivation of the Name—Beauty of the Site, p 29 Neglected Condition, p 30 A Foundation of Austin Canons—Endowments of the Abbey—The Order of Canons Regular of S Augustine, p 31 Raunton Priory subordinate to Haughmond—The Minster and its Chapels—S Mary's Light provided by Sir Richard de Leaton—Ground Plan of the Church, p 32 Fine Procession Door—The Nave a Parish Church—Tiles of the Pavement—The Transept the Tomb of the Fitz Alans, p 33 Rare Dedication of the Church to S John the Evangelist—Conventual Buildings, p 34 The Lavatory- Ruins of the Refectory, p 35 The Chapter House its Portals enriched with Images, p 36 Traces of the Dormitory—Base Court—The Infirmary, p 37 The Kitchen, p 38. The Great Hog Stye—List of the Abbots, p 39 The Conduit or Well House—Surrender of the Abbey—p 40 Pensions to the late Inmates—Grant of the Site—Commission for the Surrender—p 41 Answer of the Convent, p 43. Annuities—Corrodies, and Pensions, p 44. Osulveston Priory Founded on the Rule of Haughmond—S Mary's, Oswestry, subordinate to Haughmond—Seal of the Abbey, p 45 Description of an Austin Canons' House—The Habit and Rule, p 42. Episcopal Injunctions—Fragment of an Inventory, p 50

LILLESHULL ABBEY.

Derivation of the Name—Foundation of the Abbey for Canons of Arroaise, p. 53. Peculiarity of the Ground Plan, Approach to the Abbey, p. 54. The West Front, p. 55. The Nave—The Three Screens, p. 56. The Stalls now at Wolverhampton—The Transept—Arrangement of the Chapels—The Ritual Choir, p. 57. The Presbytery—The Sacristy—The Cloister Garth, p. 58. The fine Procession Door—East Side of the Cloister Square—The Chapter House—Sepulchral Slab of Lady Hillary de Tresse, p. 59. South Side, The Slype—The Refectory, The Entry to the Kitchen—The West Side, p. 60. Arrangements of Conventual Buildings, p. 61. Seal of the Abbey. Benefactors and Endowments—The Abbey Bede Roll, p. 62. Dean Heywood's Chantry—List of the Abbots, p. 63. Conventual Income—Grant of the Site—The Survey, p. 64.

WENLOCK PRIORY.

The beautiful Scenery and Architectural Interest of Much Wenlock, p. 75. Ancient Name—The Minster of S. Milburga—Difference between Cluniacs and Cistercians, p. 76. Dress of the Cluniac—Houses of the Order—Founders of Wenlock originally an alien Priory and Cell of La Charité, p. 77. Reyner calls it Insignis—It is made Denizen—Architectural Features of the Minster—The high Character of its Monks, p. 79. Design of Making it Cathedral—Dimensions of the Minster—Patterns of Tiles—West Front, p. 80. The Nave—Cella and Minor Choir of Novices, p. 80. Cluniac Arrangements—Chamber over the South Aisle—The Crossing—Bells sold to Wolverhampton—The Transept, p. 82. Curious Canopied Arcade—North Wing, The Sacristy over a Crypt—The Presbytery, p. 83. The Lavatory—Shrine of S. Milburga—Site of the Lady Chapel—The Cloister Garth—The Tresaunt, p. 84. Custom at Shaving—The Chapter House, p. 85. The Refectory—Peculiar Customs—West Side of the Cloister Garth, p. 86. The Court of the Infirmary—The Priors' Lodge, p. 87. The Almonry—Doles to the Poor—Relations of the Town to the Priory—Endowments of the Priory, p. 88. Fairs, Markets—Dependent Cells: Prene, St. Helen's in the Isle of Wight, and St. James,' Dudley—Paisley Colonised—Dependent Churches, p. 89. Number of Monks—The Confederation with Worcester Cathedral—The Robber Monk—Monastic Income—Grant of the Site—List of the Priors, p. 90, The last Prior's Cope—Names of the Monks at the Surrender, p. 92. Annuities and Corrodies—Number of Monks and Canons in the principal Religious Houses at the Dissolution, p. 93. Wenlock designed to be a Cathedral with Shrewsbury, 94. The Bishop of Shrewsbury. Arms of the Priory—Reflections of B. Godwin, Lord Herbert, Camden, Strype, and Stowe on the Dissolution of the Religious Houses, which had been long pending, p. 96. Petitions vainly offered for their Preservation, p. 99. Sacrilegious abuse of their Materials—Conclusion.

BOOKS BY THE SAME AUTHOR.

SACRED ARCHÆOLOGY: A Popular Dictionary of Ecclesiastical Art and Institutions, from Primitive to Modern Times, comprising Architecture, Vestments, Furniture, Arrangement, Offices, Customs, Ritual, Symbolism, Ceremonial, Traditions, Religious Orders, of the Church Catholic in all ages.—

London: L. REEVE & Co.

CATHEDRALIA: A Constitutional History of Cathedrals of the Western Church, and of the Various Dignities, Offices, and Ministries of their Members, founded on Capitular Statutes, and Illustrated from the Canon Law and Writers of repute.

London: MASTERS.

THE CONSTITUTIONS AND CANONS ECCLESIASTICAL OF THE CHURCH OF ENGLAND, referred to their Original Sources, and Illustrated with Explanatory Notes.

London: J. PARKER & Co.

CHURCH AND CONVENTUAL ARRANGEMENT, with copious References, a complete Glossary and an Index, and Illustrated by a series of Ground Plans and Plates of the Arrangements of Churches in different countries and at successive periods, and of the Conventual Plans adopted by the various orders.

London: ATCHLEY & Co.

THE ANCIENT CHURCH OF SCOTLAND (or, SCOTI MONASTICON) before the Union of the two Crowns. A History of all the Cathedral, Conventual, and Collegiate Churches and Hospitals of Scotland, with 38 Illustrations and Ground Plans.

London: VIRTUE & Co.

LOCAL WORKS, &c.,

PRINTED AND PUBLISHED BY

ADNITT & NAUNTON, THE SQUARE, SHREWSBURY.

THE GARRISONS OF SHROPSHIRE, 1641-8. Demy 4to, Cloth Antique.

THE CASTLES AND OLD MANSIONS OF SHROPSHIRE. Demy 4to, Cloth Antique.

GOUGH'S HISTORY OF MYDDLE, Co., Salop, 1701. Demy 4to, Cloth Antique. One of the most extraordinary Topographical and Genealogical Works ever printed."—Sir Thomas Phillipps (Editor of the incomplete 1834 Ed.)

THIRTEEN VIEWS OF THE CASTLE OF ST. DONAT'S, GLAMORGANSHIRE, with a Notice of the Stradling Family. Demy 4to, Cloth Antique.

THE FOUR MINSTERS ROUND THE WREKIN: Buildwas, Haughmond, Lilleshull and Wenlock, by MACKENZIE E. C. WALCOTT, B.D., F.S.A., &c., Præcentor and Prebendary of Chichester Cathedral. Demy 4to, Cloth Antique.

THE LICHEN FLORA OF GREAT BRITAIN, by Rev. W. A. LEIGHTON, F.L.S., F.B.S., Edin. Cloth, 8vo, 2nd Edition.

SKETCH OF THE PARISH OF CLEOBURY MORTIMER. Demy 8vo, with Illustrations, paper covers.

THOS. CHURCHYARD'S (THE OLD POET OF SHREWSBURY) MISERIE OF FLANDERS, &c., 1578. A fac-simile reprint Fcp. 4to, large paper. Only 70 copies printed. Half bound antique.

EXTRACTS FROM LETTERS AND SPEECHES OF SIR BALDWIN LEIGHTON, BART. Edited by his daughter Demy 8vo, paper covers.